CREDO: I BELIEVE
Teacher's Manual

CREDO: I BELIEVE

Teacher's Manual

Faith and Life Series

BOOK FIVE

Ignatius Press, San Francisco
Catholics United for the Faith, New Rochelle

Nihil Obstat: Francis J. McAree, S.T.D.
                 Censor Librorum
Imprimatur: + Joseph T. O'Keefe, D.D.
                 Vicar General, New York

Director: Rev. Msgr. Eugene Kevane, Ph.D.
Assistant Director and General Editor: Patricia I. Puccetti, M.A.
Writer: Sister Mary Ann Kirkland, I.H.M.

Catholics United for the Faith, Inc., and Ignatius Press gratefully acknowledge the guidance and assistance of Reverend Monsignor Eugene Kevane, former Director of the Pontifical Catechetical Institute, Diocese of Arlington, Virginia, in the production of this series. The series intends to implement the authentic approach in Catholic catechesis given to the Church in the recent documents of the Holy See and in particular the Conference of Joseph Cardinal Ratzinger on "Sources and Transmission of Faith".

CONTENTS

APPENDIX

Introduction

Principles

TEXT AND GRADE LEVEL

The text for the fifth grade is devoted to the Creed, which summarizes in a brief and simple way the basic truths of the faith. Fifth graders, because of their growing abilities of mind and body, are very eager to learn and to apply that learning to their daily lives. What better time than the present to help these students to delve more deeply into their faith and to apply it more completely in their lives?

CATECHESIS: NATURE AND PURPOSE

Because of your willingness to share your time and talent, you have entered more fully into one of the Church's most important and sacred duties, that of making Christ better known and loved by his children, young or old. This duty of the Church entails handing on the message of God, in its entirety and purity. You cannot mix God's message with political or social views without betraying the Divine mission. Political and social trends come and go, but the word of God is always timely. Catechesis must be based on Revelation as transmitted by the universal Teaching Authority of the Church, in its solemn or ordinary form (CT 52, cf. *Dei Filius* chapter 3). The doctrine you hand on by your teaching is received by your students as it truly is, the very Word of God, accepted as it is taught, namely, on the authority of God revealing (cf. 1 Th 2:13).

This teacher's manual is designed to help you in this important work of handing on the living and unchanging Word of God.

Catechetics, according to the *General Catechetical Directory*, is the form of the ministry of the word of God, "which is intended to make men's faith become living, conscious, and active, through the light of instruction" (GCD 17). This instruction presupposes that the student already knows and believes in at least the basics of the gospel as taught by the Church. A good way to determine the depth of your students' knowledge of the faith is to ask them the basic questions listed in the Appendix. It will then be easier to know which students require more fundamental instruction.

THE CATECHIST: CHRIST'S INSTRUMENT

If teaching religion seems like a big task, that is only because it *is* a big task! But don't get worried! As Pope John Paul II said in *Catechesi Tradendae*: "It is Christ . . . who is taught . . . and it is Christ alone who teaches" (CT 6). This statement means that you are Christ's instrument; through you he will spread his message. You have a very important role in faithfully passing on the message of the gospel, the constant, unchanging message: Jesus Christ, the only begotten Son of God, made man. On the other hand, you also have the assurance that God is going to help you every step of the way in proclaiming his message. You, too, have the guarantee given to the apostles: "I will be with you always even to the end of the world" (cf. Mt 28:20).

You are also very important because it is the living catechist, the living example, who gets the message across. No matter which text you use, no matter which method you choose, it will be the message you present, your living of the gospel, your likeness to Christ that will be most important in bringing your students closer to Christ (cf. GCD 71). Consequently, you need to prepare yourself for the task, always confident that if you do your part God will do his. The best way to prepare yourself is to pray, to study, to pray, to plan, and to pray.

THE ROLE OF THE PARENTS: THE FIRST CATECHISTS

The family provides the first and irreplaceable introduction to Christian faith and practice for any child. Parents are the first instructors of their children. The instruction in the faith, which starts from the earliest age, should include not only the parents' good Christian example, but also a formation in prayer and an explanation and review of what their children have learned about the faith from methodical religious instruction and liturgical events (CT 68). (In some situations where the children attend neither a Catholic school nor a CCD class because these are not available or are inadequate, the parents [or the grandparents] are the *only* source of catechetical instruction. If this situation is yours, God bless your efforts and may this series help you in the children's formation in Christ.)

Parental cooperation is very important to a teacher's success as a catechist. You should try to involve parents in their children's instruction: sharing with them the program and methods you are using, consulting them about better ways to reach their children or to help with problems that may arise. Let the parents know that you are there to help them fulfill their duties in forming and educating their children in Christ (cf. GCD 78, 79).

Practicalities

LESSON PLANNING

Lesson planning is very important for an organized and successful teacher. It helps you cover all the material systematically in the time that you have available.

The first step in planning is to make an overview of everything you want to teach during the year. For example, there are thirty chapters in the fifth grade text, but suppose you are in a CCD program and you are going to have only twenty-eight classes during the school year. You will need to plan which lessons you can combine and which lessons you might want to expand over two or three weeks. If you have the students every weekday, the overview is also helpful to you in scheduling what needs to be covered every week so that nothing is left out or covered too quickly. Included in the Appendix is a chart to help you plan your course for the year.

The second step is to plan the daily lesson so as to reach the students on as many levels as possible. The *General Catechetical Directory* #70 mentions *experience, imagination, memory,* and *intelligence* as different faculties of the children that should be active in the task of learning. A good lesson plan will involve all of these faculties.

RECOMMENDED CATECHETICAL SOURCES

Catechism of Christian Doctrine, published by order of Pope St. Pius X, trans. Rev. Msgr. Eugene Kevane (Arlington, Va., Center for Family Catechetics, 1980). (The questions in the children's texts are from this catechism.)

Hardon, John A., S.J., *The Catholic Catechism* (New York: Doubleday and Co., Inc., 1975), 623 pages.

Lawler, Ronald, O.F.M., Cap., Donald W. Wuerl, and Thomas Comerford Lawler, editors, *The Teaching of Christ: A Catholic Catechism for Adults*, 2nd ed. (Huntington: Our Sunday Visitor, Inc., 1983), 640 pages.

The Roman Catechism, translated and annotated by Rev. Robert I. Bradley, S.J. and Rev. Msgr. Eugene Kevane (Boston: St. Paul Editions, 1985), 586 pages.

Sharing the Light of Faith, National Conference of Catholic Bishops (Washington, D.C.: United States Catholic Conference, 1979).

Vatican Council II: The Conciliar and Post Conciliar Documents, gen. ed. Austin Flannery, O.P. (New York: Costello Publishing, 1975).

Vatican Council II, More Post Conciliar Documents, gen ed. Austin Flannery, O.P. (New York: Costello Publishing, 1982). (This volume includes *Catechesi Tradendae*, and the *General Catechetical Directory*, both vital documents for the Catechist.)

POINTS ON TEACHING CHILDREN

1. The first thing necessary for successfully communicating the message of the gospel

is to have a genuine love for the gospel and for your students; all else flows from this love. A genuine love consists of desiring the greatest good for your students, which necessitates maintaining a fair and consistent discipline. Your task is not merely to teach a subject matter but to form children in the image of Christ. State clearly your requirements and the reasons behind them. Do not let the rules slip. If you have made something a policy stick to it! Jesus himself was gentle but firm.

2. Learn the names of your students as quickly as possible. This small effort will help you maintain discipline and let your students know that you care enough about them to remember who they are.

3. Try to call on everyone, not just on those students who volunteer; in this way everyone remains attentive and the shy students have an opportunity to come out of themselves.

4. Give clear directions for assignments. For example, do the first part of the assignment with the children or do the assignments or activities yourself beforehand so that you are familiar with the problems your students might have. Walk around the classroom so that you can give individual attention to those students having difficulties.

5. If you notice a normally attentive student not paying attention, find out what the problem is and be willing to take the time (outside of class time if possible) to help or find someone who can.

6. When using the chalkboard, remember to start at the left-hand side. Skipping around is extremely confusing for the students.

7. Overplan. It is all right if you run out of time; it can be a disaster if you run out of material to teach.

8. Review the lesson with your students at the end of the class period and review the lesson again at the beginning of the next class before starting the new lesson. Repetition *is* the mother of learning.

Suggested Introductory Lesson

Aims:

To find out how much the students know and understand about their faith; to get to know the students and to familiarize them with class content and procedure.

Materials Needed:

Student texts and activity books, folders with students' names on them (optional), name tags (optional), seating chart (optional), game or quiz (see the Appendix for game), paper and pencils.

Procedure

1. Pray.

2. Play a name game to learn your students' names, or give them name tags, or make a seating chart beforehand.

3. Hand out text and activity books. (You might supply your students with folders in which to keep books, papers and pencils.)

4. Ask the basic catechism questions from the Appendix (p. 93), either in the form of a quiz or a game.

5. Introduce the subject the students will be studying during the year.

6. Assign the students Chapter 1 of the textbook to read. (You might find it more practical to have the reading assignment read and discussed during the class covering the particular chapter rather than assign it as homework).

7. Pray.

PART ONE

God,
The Father of All

CHAPTER 1

I Believe

Background Reading for the Teacher:

Lawler, pp. 29—36.[1]
Hardon, pp. 29—41.[2]

Aims:

The students should be able to explain the two different aspects of faith (the act of believing and the content of belief); to recite the Apostles' Creed from memory and to list the twelve articles of faith contained in the Creed; and to define the words and answer the catechism questions at the end of Chapter 1.

Materials Needed:

Paper (butcher paper for "Creed scroll"), crayons, cardboard clock face (or draw the clock on the chalkboard), poster board, scissors, magic marker, Bibles for students and teacher.

Activities

1. Use a "clock" to memorize the 12 doctrines of the Creed.

   1. God the Father, Creator
   2. Jesus Christ, only Son
   3. Jesus' conception by the Holy Spirit, birth from the Virgin Mary
   4. Passion, death and burial
   5. Descent into hell and Resurrection
   6. Ascension and glory of Christ
   7. Judgment of all the living and dead
   8. Holy Spirit
   9. Holy Catholic Church; Communion of Saints
   10. Forgiveness of sins
   11. Resurrection of the body
   12. Everlasting life

---

[1] Ronald Lawler, O.F.M. Cap., ed., *The Teaching of Christ*, 2nd ed. (Huntington: Our Sunday Visitor, Inc., 1983).

[2] John A. Hardon, S.J., *The Catholic Catechism* (Garden City: Doubleday and Company, 1975).

2. Write the Apostles' Creed on a poster board and cut it into twelve strips, each strip with an article of the Creed on it; have the students put it together like a puzzle.

3. Draw pictures of the articles of the Apostles' Creed (or have the whole class draw a Creed scroll).

4. Dramatize how the students might exercise their gift / virtue of faith.

5. Read Scripture quotes that show examples of faith: for example Gen 15:1−6 on Abraham's faith, and Lk 1:26−38 on Mary's faith.

6. Have a contest to see who can find the most occurrences of the word "faith" in a book of the New Testament.

7. Have the students write a "journal" on how they or their families live the gift of faith.

Lesson Plan for a One-day Presentation

1. Pray.

2. Read Gen 15:1−6 and Lk 1:26−38 and discuss Abraham's and Mary's faith.

3. Ask the question, "What is faith?"
   a. A gift from God that gives us the power to believe what he tells us about himself and his creation.
   b. The truths of God's revelation to us, which are summarized in the Creed.

4. Say the Apostles' Creed together.

5. Have the students pick out the twelve articles of the Apostles' Creed. Write the articles on the board as they say them, or have them put the doctrine around the "Catechetical Clock" (see Activities, above), or use the Activity Book for Chapter 1.

6. Have the whole class or individual students make a "Creed scroll" illustrating the twelve articles. (Butcher paper works well for this project.)

7. Assign the students to read Chapter 2, pp. 13−17. Make an assignment sheet consisting of the catechism questions and Words to Know at the end of the Chapter (or you might use the Activity Book as a homework assignment, or have them write a paragraph on how they or their families live their faith).

8. Review the material covered in class.

9. Pray the Apostles' Creed as a closing prayer.

Suggested Schedule for a Five-day Presentation

1. Introduction
   See Suggested Introductory Lesson

2. Faith: gift of God, content of revelation
   Aim: to explain the different aspects of faith.
   Activities: see activities 4, 5, 6, and 7, above.

3. Creed: summary of the truths of revelation
   Aim: to recite the Apostles' Creed from memory and to list the twelve articles of faith.
   Activities: see activities 1, 2, and 3, above.

4. Creed (continued)
   Aim: see aim for day 3, and define the words and answer the catechism questions at the end of Chapter 1.
   Activities: see activities 1, 2, and 3, above; a review game, see the Appendix.

5. Review
   Aim: to review the material covered this week.
   Activities: review games, quiz.

CHAPTER 2

The Trinity

Background Reading for the Teacher:

Lawler, pp. 36−42.
Hardon, pp. 63−67.

Aims:

The student should be able to explain the basic doctrine of the Trinity, at the same time understanding that it is a mystery that cannot be fully explained; to list the attributes of God; to define the words *mystery*, *Trinity*, *nature* and *Person*; and to answer the catechism questions at the end of the chapter.

Materials Needed:

Bibles, real or paper three-leaf clover or shamrock (optional).

Activities

1. As a missionary, St. Patrick used the shamrock to explain that there are three Persons in one God. Tell the story about St. Patrick using the shamrock to teach about the Trinity (you might want to bring in a ''shamrock'' of your own).

2. Tell the story about St. Augustine walking along a beach trying to understand the mystery of the Trinity. As he was walking along he met a little boy digging a hole in the sand. When Augustine asked the boy what he was doing he answered that he was digging a hole to put the sea into. Augustine laughed and said that that was impossible. The little boy answered that it was more possible for him to put the sea in that little hole than it was for a human mind to understand completely the mysteries of the faith, and with that the boy vanished.

3. Have the students pretend they are teachers. How would they teach the Trinity to their students?

4. Read New Testament quotes about the Trinity (Mk 1:10−11; Mt 28:19; Jn 16:5−15).

5. Discuss picture on p. 15 in the text. Why are the Persons of the Trinity portrayed in this way? Are there three Gods? Are the three Persons "parts" of One God?

6. Read and discuss Is 6:3 (God is all-holy); Am 5:8 (God is almighty); Ps 139 (God is all-knowing); Rev 4:8 (God is eternal); Ps 102:25−27 (God is unchanging); Ps 139:7−10 (God is all-present). (You can make it into a contest, "Who can find the quote first?")

Lesson Plan for a One-day Presentation

1. Pray.

2. Briefly review the last lesson.

3. Tell the story about St. Patrick and the shamrock, or St. Augustine and the little boy.

4. Read New Testament quotes about the Trinity. (See the Activity Book on this chapter. You could use it here or as an assignment.)

5. Explain the doctrine of the Trinity. (Use the diagram from the activities section above, or ask and discuss the questions on the Trinity in the text.)

6. Look at the picture on p. 15 in the text and discuss it.

7. Have the students teach one another about the Trinity.

8. Have the students list the attributes of God mentioned in Chapter 2; explain each one.

9. Review the content of this lesson.

10. Assign the students to read Chapter 3, pp. 19−21. (Make an assignment sheet with the catechism questions and Words to Know.) Have them write a paragraph on

how they can pray to and love each Person of the Trinity.

11. Pray the Glory Be to the Father as a closing prayer.

Suggested Schedule for a Five-day Presentation

1. God's perfections: All-Holy, Almighty, All-Knowing

   Aim: to list and explain the attributes of God.

   Activities: review game to go over last week's material; see activity 6.

2. God's perfections: Eternal, Unchanging, All-Present

   Aim: see day 1.

   Activities: see activity 6.

3. God's nature: the Mystery of the Trinity

   Aim: to explain the basic doctrine of the Trinity, at the same time making them understand that it is a mystery.

   Activities: see activities 1−5.

4. God's Nature: the Mystery of the Trinity

   Aim: see day 3.

   Activities: see day 3, and define words and answer the catechism questions at the end of Chapter 2.

5. Review

   Aim: to review the material covered this week.

   Activities: review games, quiz.

Notes:

CHAPTER 3

Creator of Heaven and Earth

Background Reading for the Teacher:

Lawler, pp. 43−54.
Hardon, pp. 68−83.

Aims:

The students should be able to define the word *create* in order to explain how they are able to come to a knowledge of God through his creation; to appreciate what God has done for them by listing some of the things he has given them; and to tell how they should use God's creation to serve him.

Materials Needed:

Old magazines, scissors, glue, paper, Bibles, pencils.

Activities

1. Read aloud and discuss St. Augustine's poem on p. 21 in the text.

2. Discuss the difference between God's creativity and man's creativity. (Use a funny example such as, ''How would God make a pink hippopotamus and how would you?'')

3. Make a collage of some of the things God has created.

4. Take a short field trip just outside the building or to a nearby park. Have the students find examples of pattern and order around them that would indicate an intelligent Creator.

5. Read Scripture quotes on God's love in creating the world for us (Ps 23; Ps 139; Mt 6:25−34; Mt 18:12−14).

6. Have the students list some of the things God has given to them, for example, parents, health, talents.

7. Write a prayer thanking God for his love in creating the world for us.

8. Have the students list some ways they can use God's creation well (see Mt 25:14−30, the parable of the talents).

Lesson Plan for a One-day Presentation

1. Pray.

2. Briefly review the material from Chapter 2.

3. Discuss how God created the world out of nothing, with complete freedom and because of his great love.

4. Read Scripture quotes on God's love in creating and sustaining us (Ps 139 or Mt 6:25−34).

5. Have the students list some of the things that God has given them.

6. Have the students write a prayer thanking God for all the good things he has given them.

7. Read aloud and discuss St. Augustine's poem (p. 21 in the text).

8. Take the students outside for a few minutes. Have them find examples of order or design that would point to the Creator (or have them do the assignment in the activity book, or talk about how we can know God from creation).

9. Review the material covered during this lesson.

10. Assign Chapter 4, pp. 22−25, with a question sheet (assignment in the Activity Book if not already used in class).

11. Pray.

Suggested Schedule for a Five-day Presentation

1. Creation: God's creating from nothing, with complete freedom, out of love
   Aim: to define the word *create* and answer the questions at the end of Chapter 3.
   Activities: see activities 2 and 3, above.

2. Creation: man's discovery of God through creation
   Aim: to explain how men and women are able to come to a knowledge of God through his creation.
   Activities: see activities 1 and 4, above.

3. Providence: God's sustaining of creation
   Aim: to appreciate what God has done for us by listing some of the things we have received from him.
   Activities: see activities 5 and 6.

4. Stewardship: man's responsibility and gratitude for creation
   Aim: to think of ways that the students can use God's creation to serve him.
   Activities: see activities 7 and 8.

5. Review
   Aim: to review the material covered this week.
   Activities: review games, show and tell, quiz.

Notes:

CHAPTER 4

Realm of the Angels

Background Reading for the Teacher:

Lawler, pp. 54−55, 74−76.
Hardon, pp. 83−90.

Aims:

The students should be able to define the nature of angels; to explain why there are good and bad angels; to tell some of the stories about angels in Scripture; to say the prayer to St. Michael; to pray to and listen to their guardian angels.

Materials:

Bibles, props for angel skits (see Appendix, p. 98), copies of songs: ''Ye Watchers and Ye Holy Ones'' and ''Hail Holy Queen''.

Activities

1. Read Scripture quotes about angels (Lk 1:26−38; Acts 5:17−81; Acts 10:30ff.; Acts 12:1−11; Rev 12:7−17) and devils (Lk 4:1−13; Lk 8:26−39).

2. Look at the picture on p. 24 in the text and read the account from Acts 12:1−11 about St. Peter's deliverance from prison.

3. Dramatize how angels guard and guide their charges and how the students should behave toward angels.

4. Tell stories about angels, for example, the angel of Portugal who prepared Lucia, Jacinta, and Francisco for the appearance of Our Lady of Fatima.

5. Sing ''Ye Watchers and Ye Holy Ones'' or ''Hail Holy Queen''.

Lesson Plan for a One-day Presentation

1. Pray.

2. Briefly review last week's lesson.

3. Look at the picture on p. 24 in the text and read Acts 12:1−11.

4. Discuss the nature of angels and their role as God's messengers and guardians.

5. Read Scripture quotes on angels.

6. Talk about the trial of angels and the choice of some of them not to love or serve God (read Rev 12:7−17).

7. Discuss the reality of Satan and the bad angels (read Lk 4:1−13; Lk 8:26−39).

8. Dramatize how angels guard and guide the people God puts in their charge.

9. Review today's lesson.

10. Assign Chapter 5, pp. 26−28, and the assignment for Chapter 4 in the Activity Book.

11. Pray the Prayer to St. Michael, p. 23, in the text.

**Suggested Schedule for a
Five-day Presentation**

1. The angelic nature
   Aim: to define the nature of angels.
   Activities: see activities 4 and 5.

2. The angels' test (angels and devils)
   Aim: to explain why there are good and bad angels.
   Activities: see activity 5; read Rev 12:7−17 and discuss.

3. The angels' presence in Scripture
   Aim: to tell some of the stories about angels in Scripture.
   Activities: see activities 1 and 2.

4. The angels' role in human affairs
   Aim: to pray to and listen to our guardian angels.
   Activities: see activity 3, answer and discuss catechism questions and Words to Know at the end of Chapter 4.

5. Review
   Aim: to review the material covered this week.
   Activities: review game, quiz.

Notes:

CHAPTER 5

Made in His Image

Background Reading for the Teacher:

Lawler, pp. 56—65.
Hardon, pp. 91—99, 102—107.

Aims:

The students should be able to define the *nature of man*, the *immortality of the soul*, *free will*, *grace*; to describe the state of original justice; and to value every human life as coming from God.

Materials Needed:

Bibles, book or tape on Blessed Margaret of Castello, props for skit.

Activities

1. Read Scripture quotes on man's nature, for example, Gen 1:26—2:3; Sir 17:1—12; Ps 8:5—7.

2. Read, or play the tape of, the story of Blessed Margaret of Castello.[1]

3. Dramatize the creation of man and woman.

4. Discuss the supernatural gift of sanctifying grace; the preternatural gifts of immortality of the body, infused knowledge and integrity; and the natural gifts of body and soul.

5. Look at the chart on p. 11 of the Activity Book and discuss man's nature in its relationship to the spiritual and material realms.

Lesson Plan for a One-day Presentation

1. Pray.

2. Briefly review the material from Chapter 4.

3. Read the story of man's creation from Genesis; dramatize the episode.

4. Discuss the gifts that Adam and Eve had in the state of original justice.

---

[1] W. R. Bonniwell, *The Life of Blessed Margaret of Castello* (Elmwood Park: I.D.E.A., 1979). Gerald Hofman, "The Life of Bl. Margaret of Castello, O.P." (Montvale: Keep the Faith, Inc., n.d.).

5. Tell the story of Blessed Margaret of Castello (or play the tape); then discuss how every person whether small or weak, old or unborn, handicapped or sick is precious in God's eyes.

6. Look at the chart on p. 11 of the Activity Book and talk about man's nature in relationship to the spiritual and material realms of being.

7. Review the material covered in this lesson.

8. Assign Chapter 6, pp. 29−32, and the assignment for Chapter 5 in the Activity Book (if you have not already done it in class).

9. Pray.

Suggested Schedule for a Five-day Presentation

1. Man's nature: body and soul
   Aim: to define the nature of man.
   Activities: see activities 3 and 5.

2. Our first parents
   Aim: to define the nature of man.
   Activities: see activity 1.

3. Man's original justice
   Aim: to describe the state of original justice.
   Activities: see activity 4.

4. The value of human life
   Aim: to value every human life as coming from God.
   Activities: see activity 2.

5. Review
   Aim: to review the week's material.
   Activities: review games, quiz.

Notes:

CHAPTER 6

The Fall from Grace

Background Reading for the Teacher:

Lawler, pp. 99–102.   Gen 3.
Hardon, pp. 66–74.

Aims:

The students should be able to tell the story of the testing of man (Gen 3); to explain the state of original justice and the effects of original sin for Adam and Eve, and for their descendants; to explain the effects of baptism on our souls; to tell God's promise to Adam and Eve of a Savior and the Savior's Mother who would be conceived without sin; and to come to a Christian understanding of suffering.

Materials Needed:

Bibles, paper, pencils, crayons, picture or statue of the Immaculate Conception.

Activities

1. Read and/or dramatize the temptation and fall of man (Gen 3).

2. Draw pictures of the Garden of Eden before and after the original sin.

3. Show a picture or statue of the Immaculate Conception. Why is Mary standing on the serpent's head? Why does the serpent have an apple in its jaws? (See Gen 3:15.)

4. Discuss and complete the chart on p. 13 in the Activity Book.

Lesson Plan for a One-day Presentation

1. Pray.

2. Review all the gifts Adam and Eve had before the fall.

3. Dramatize the fall of man (Gen 3).

4. Tell the students of the effects of the original sin on Adam and Eve and on the human race.

5. Draw a picture of the Garden of Eden before and after the fall.

6. Read and discuss the promise of a Savior given to Adam and Eve. (Gen 3:15). Show them a picture of the Immaculate Conception if you wish; see activities section above.

7. Talk about how baptism removes original sin (you might want to use p. 13 of the Activity Book here).

8. Review the material covered today, and go over the word and catechism questions at the end of the chapter.

9. Assign Chapter 7, pp. 33–34 (and p. 13 in the Activity Book if not already used in class).

10. Pray.

Suggested Schedule for a Five-day Presentation

1. Original justice
   Aim: to explain the state of justice in which man was created.
   Activity: discuss original justice and have the students draw a picture of the Garden of Eden before the fall of man.

2. Original sin
   Aim: to explain the effects of the original sin for Adam and Eve and their descendants; to tell the story of man's temptation and fall.
   Activities: see activities 1 and 2.

3. God's promise
   Aim: to tell God's promise to Adam and Eve of a Savior and of the Savior's Mother who would be conceived without sin.
   Activities: see activity 3; read Gen 3:15.

4. Baptism
   Aim: to explain the effects of baptism on our souls.
   Activities: see activity 4.

5. Review
   Aim: to review this week's material.
   Activities: review game, quiz.

Notes:

CHAPTER 7

The Chosen People

Background Reading for the Teacher:

Lawler, pp. 76—77.
Gen 12—50.

Aims:

The students should be able to tell the stories of Abraham, Isaac, Jacob, and Joseph.

Materials Needed:

Props for dramatization, paper, crayons, Bibles (if you choose a film strip: projector, tape or record player, screen, extension cord).

Activities

1. Dramatize the sacrifice of Isaac (Gen 22: 1—19).

2. Read or dramatize the story of Jacob's trickery (Gen 27).

3. Complete the word search in the Activity Book on p. 14.

4. Draw pictures of the sacrifice of Isaac, or Jacob's trick to get his father's blessing, or selling Joseph into slavery (or make a "family scroll" for Abraham's family).

5. Read or dramatize the story of Joseph (Gen 37; 39; 41; 45).

6. Show filmstrips on the patriarchs.

Lesson Plan for a One-day Presentation

1. Pray.

2. Review the condition of the human race after the fall of Adam and Eve.

3. Tell the students how God chose a special people to prepare mankind for the Savior he had promised.

4. Read the account of Isaac's sacrifice (Gen 22:1—19); discuss the greatness of Abraham's faith and obedience. Who else can you think of that trusted and obeyed God as Abraham did? (Mary).

5. Dramatize the story of Jacob's trick to get his father's special blessing (or show a film strip).

6. Tell the story of Joseph (Gen 37; 39; 41; 45).

7. Have the students make a "scroll of Abraham's family" with drawings of the stories of Abraham, Isaac, Jacob, and Joseph (or have the students work individually on their favorite story).

8. Review the material covered during this lesson.

9. Assign Chapter 8, pp. 35−38, and p. 14 in the Activity Book.

10. Pray.

**Suggested Schedule for a
Five-day Presentation**

1. Abraham
   Aim: to tell the story of Abraham and explain the importance of faith in God.

Activities: read Gen 12:1−9 and Lk 1:26−38 and discuss the faith shown by Abraham and Mary. How can we practice our faith like they did?

2. Isaac
   Aim: to tell the story of Abraham and Isaac.
   Activities: see activity 1.

3. Jacob
   Aim: to tell the story of Jacob.
   Activities: see activity 2.

4. Joseph
   Aim: to tell the story of Joseph.
   Activities: see activity 5.

5. Review
   Aim: to review this week's material.
   Activities: see activities 4 and 6, quiz.

Notes:

CHAPTER 8

Moses Leads God's People

Background Reading for the Teacher:

Ex 1–12; 14.

Aims:

The students should be able to tell the story of Moses and the Exodus; to explain how the Passover foreshadows the Mystery of Redemption: Christ's suffering, death and Resurrection; to explain how the crossing of the Red Sea foreshadows the sacrament of baptism.

Materials Needed:

Bibles, paper, pencils, crayons, props for dramatization. If you should choose to reenact the Passover meal: grape drink, matzos or saltine crackers, chopped apples and nuts with cinnamon representing the mortar the Jews had to make for Pharaoh, parsley or horseradish dipped in salt water representing the bitterness of the Jews' slavery and their tears, and roasted lamb. If you want to simplify the reenactment you could pretend to have a lamb or make a cake in the shape of a lamb. Have the students bring these things or help make these things in class.

Activities

1. Draw a picture of Moses being saved by Pharaoh's daughter (Ex 2).

2. Use the activity on p. 15 in the Activity Book.

3. Have a contest to see who can find all ten plagues in Exodus first (Ex 7–12).

4. Dramatize Moses' call (Ex 3).

5. Reenact a "Passover Meal" and discuss how it relates to the Last Supper and the Mass.

6. Show a filmstrip on Moses.

7. Read Ps 105 on p. 38 in the text as a review of salvation history from Abraham to Moses.

Lesson Plan for a One-day Presentation

1. Pray.

2. Review the material covered in the last lesson.

3. Read Ex 1 and 2 or tell the story of the Jews' slavery and Moses' adoption by Pharaoh's daughter.

4. Draw a picture of Pharaoh's daughter saving Moses from the Nile.

5. Dramatize Moses' call (Ex 3).

6. Tell the students about Pharaoh's stubbornness. Have a contest to see who can find all ten plagues in Ex 7—12.

7. Read the instruction for the Passover Meal (Ex 12). Discuss how the events of the Passover foreshadow the Last Supper and Jesus' suffering and death.

8. Tell the story of the crossing of the Red Sea. How does this event foreshadow the sacrament of baptism?

9. Review by reading Ps 105 on p. 38 in the text.

10. Assign p. 15 in the Activity Book and Chapter 9, pp. 39—41 in the text.

11. Pray.

Suggested Schedule for a Five-day Presentation

1. Moses' birth and adoption
   Aim: to tell the story of Moses.
   Activities: see activities 1 and 6.

2. Moses' call
   Aim: to tell the story of Moses.
   Activities: see activity 4.

3. The ten plagues
   Aim: to tell the story of the Exodus.
   Activities: see activity 3; prepare for activity 5.

4. The Passover
   Aim: to tell the story of the Exodus; to explain how the Passover foreshadows the Mysteries of Redemption.
   Activities: see activity 5.

5. Crossing of the Red Sea
   Aim: to tell the story of the Exodus; to explain how the crossing of the Red Sea foreshadows the sacrament of baptism.
   Activities: read the account of the crossing of the Red Sea, Ex 14, and discuss how it foreshadows baptism; review with activities 2 and 7.

Notes:

CHAPTER 9

The Forming of God's People

Background Reading for the Teacher:

Ex 16; 17; 20:1−21;
25:10−12; 32.

Dt 5.
1 Sam 8; 2 Sam 7.

Aims:

The students should be able to tell the story of the Chosen People in the desert and the covenant on Mt. Sinai; to list the Ten Commandments from memory; to know a little bit about the kings of Israel, especially King David.

Materials Needed:

Copies of the model of the Ark of the Covenant (see the Appendix), paper, pencils, Bibles, questions on the Ten Commandments.

Activities

1. Make a model Ark of the Covenant (see the Appendix, p. 101).

2. From paper make "tablets" with the Ten Commandments on them.

3. Play "Bible Baseball" and "pitch" questions on the Ten Commandments (see the Appendix, p. 95).

4. Draw a picture of Moses receiving the Ten Commandments and the people worshipping the golden calf.

5. Use the activity on pp. 16−17 in the Activity Book.

Lesson Plan for a One-day Presentation

1. Pray.

2. Review the material from the last lesson.

3. Show a completed model of the Ark of the Covenant. Tell the story of how it came to be made and what was contained inside it. (You could have the students make their own models at this time or send the models home as an assignment.)

4. Have the students read the account of the apostasy of Israel (Ex 31:18−32:35); discuss God's mercy and Moses' prayer for sinners. Shouldn't we pray for sinners too?

5. Have the students make "Ten Commandment Tablets" (if they haven't made the model of the Ark).

6. Play "Bible Baseball" making up questions on the Ten Commandments as a review.

7. Assign pp. 16−17 in the Activity Book and Chapter 10, pp. 42−43.

8. Pray.

Suggested Schedule for a Five-Day Presentation

1. The Chosen People in the desert
   Aim: to tell the story of the Chosen People in the desert.
   Activities: read Ex 15:22−17:7 or tell the story. How are the Chosen People acting? How does God respond? Do we act as these people do? How should we act?

2. The covenant on Mt. Sinai
   Aim: to tell the story of the covenant between God and the Israelites on Mt. Sinai.
   Activities: see activities 1 and 4.

3. The Ten Commandments
   Aim: to list the Ten Commandments from memory.
   Activities: see activities 2 and 3.

4. The kings of Israel
   Aim: to skim the history of the kings of Israel with special attention to King David.
   Activities: briefly outline the time between Moses and the prophets; read 2 Sam 7 and discuss the promise given to David. How is it fulfilled in Jesus?

5. Review
   Aim: to review the material covered this week.
   Activities: see activity 5.

Notes:

CHAPTER 10

The Words of the Prophets

Background Reading for the Teacher:

Lawler, p. 78.
Is 7:14; 52:13−53:12.

Aims:

The students should be able to define the word *prophet*; to appreciate, by not being afraid to witness to the faith to others, their "being different from everyone else", because they are members of God's Chosen People, the Catholic Church; to list and explain the three main messages of all the prophets; to give some examples of how God prepared the way for his Son's Incarnation through the messages of the prophets.

Materials Needed:

Bibles, paper, pencils.

Activities

1. Complete the assignment from p. 18 in the Activity Book.

2. Discuss how the Chosen People wanted to be "like everybody else". Are we like the Chosen People, ashamed because we are different from those who don't believe in God? What can we do to remain faithful to God when people around us make fun of us because we believe in God and follow his Commandments?

3. Read Scripture quotes from Isaiah on Christ's birth from the Virgin Mary (Is 7:14), and the Suffering Servant songs (especially Is 52:13−53:12) on Christ's suffering and death for the salvation of mankind.

4. Play a review game (see the Appendix).

5. Write "prophecies" on the three basic messages of all the prophets (worship God only, worship him sincerely, practice justice toward others).

Lesson Plan for a One-day Presentation

1. Pray.

2. Review the material covered in the last lesson.

3. Ask the students, "What is a prophet?" Discuss how the prophet is not just a fore-teller but also a messenger of God, correcting

and teaching God's truth even when it isn't popular. Other questions you might ask would be, "Do we have prophets now?" "Who are they?" (Pope John Paul II, bishops in union with the Pope, Mother Teresa of Calcutta. . . .) "Are we called to be prophets to those around us?" "How can we be messengers of God's word?"

4. Three basic messages that can be found in all the prophets are that we must worship God alone, worship him with our whole heart, and be just to our neighbor. Have the students pretend that God called them to prophesy to their fellow students. Have them choose one of the three basic messages and write a "prophecy" on that subject. (The object is to help the students understand that the messages for the Chosen People in the Old Testament are still applicable to today's Chosen People.) Have the students read their "prophecies" to the class.

5. The prophets not only corrected the people for their sins, they also prepared the way for Christ's coming. Isaiah prepared the way for Christ by foretelling that he would be born of a virgin (see Is 7:14) and that he would come to free mankind from sin by suffering and dying (see Is 52:13—53:12). Have the students read these quotes aloud and have them tell you how Jesus fulfilled these prophecies. (Encourage students to find the fulfillment in the Gospels.)

6. Have a review activity, a game, or a quiz. (Since this Chapter ends the first part of the text you might want to set aside a class period for reviewing and/or testing.)

7. Assign Chapter 11, pp. 47—49.

8. Pray.

Suggested Schedule for a Five-day Presentation

1. Prophets' messages and suffering
   Aim: to define the word *prophet*; to explain the prophets' job; and to list the three main messages of the prophets.
   Activities: see 3 and 4 in the lesson plan for a one-day presentation.

2. People's unfaithfulness and punishment
   Aim: to appreciate their "being different" because they belong to Jesus Christ.
   Activities: see activity 2; read 2 Chron 36:11—23 and discuss.

3. Messianic prophecies and preparation
   Aim: to give some examples of how God prepared the way for his Son's Incarnation through the messages of the prophets.
   Activities: see activity 3.

4. Review of Chapters 1—10
   Aim: to review the material covered in Chapters 1—10.
   Activities: review games.

5. Test covering Chapters 1—10
   Aim: to review the material covered in Chapters 1—10.
   Activities: Give a test covering Chapters 1—10. You may wish to devote a whole week to reviewing the material covered in the course thus far.

Notes:

PART TWO

God the Son,
The Redeemer

CHAPTER 11

In the Fullness of Time

Background Reading for the Teacher:

Lawler, pp. 81−82, 97−102, 109−110.

Hardon, pp. 150−160.
Lk 1.

Aims:

The students should be able to list the events that take place in Lk 1; to explain the doctrine of the Immaculate Conception.

Materials Needed:

Bibles, props, Activity Books.

Activities

1. Review game on Chapters 1−10 (or review the tests you gave them).

2. Read Chapter 11 or Lk 1 and discuss.

3. Draw pictures of the events in Lk 1, especially the Annunciation.

4. Do the assignment in the Activity Book, pp. 19−20.

5. Read Q. 44 on p. 49 in the text and discuss.

6. Explain Mary's sinlessness. Help the students understand that God created Mary so that she would be worthy of the special privilege of being the Mother of God. This special favor of the Immaculate Conception was given in anticipation of the acts of Redemption to be accomplished by her Son, Jesus.

Lesson Plan for a One-day Presentation

1. Pray.

2. Review salvation history from Abraham to the prophets. (If you gave a test, use it as a review.)

3. Read Chapter 11 aloud.

4. Draw Zechariah and the angel, the Annunciation, and the Visitation.

5. Complete the assignment on pp. 19–20 in the Activity Book.

6. Review original sin and God's promise of a Savior. Gen 3:15.

7. Discuss the catechism question on p. 49.

8. Review the material covered in this lesson.

9. Assign Chapter 12, pp. 50–53. Make a question sheet with Words to Know and the catechism questions.

10. Pray.

Suggested Schedule for a Five-day Presentation

1. Fullness of time
   Aim: to review the events from Abraham to the prophets.
   Activities: see activity 1.

2. Annunciation
   Aim: to tell the story of the Annunciation and the events leading up to it.
   Activities: see activities 2 and 3.

3. Visitation and Magnificat
   Aim: to tell the story of the Visitation and to explain the significance of the Magnificat.
   Activities: see activities 2, 3, and 4.

4. Immaculate Conception
   Aim: to explain the doctrine of the Immaculate Conception.
   Activities: see activities 5 and 6.

5. Review
   Aim: to review this week's material.
   Activities: review game, quiz.

Notes:

CHAPTER 12

Born in the City of David

Background Reading for the Teacher:

Lawler, pp. 81—96.   Mt 1:18—2:18.
Hardon, pp. 108—149.   Lk 2:1—38.

Aims:

The student should be able to recount the events of Christ's conception, birth, and infancy; to explain the doctrine of the Incarnation.

Materials Needed:

Bibles, props, paper, crayons, filmstrip (optional).

Activities

1. Read and discuss Chapter 12 in class, especially concerning the wonder of the Incarnation.

2. Dramatize Mt 1:18—2:18.

3. Make a drawing of the Presentation (see Lk 2:22—38).

4. Show a filmstrip on Christ's Incarnation and birth or a filmstrip on the Joyful Mysteries of the Rosary.

5. Read and carefully explain the catechism questions on p. 53.

6. Make a ''matchbox nativity'' (see the Appendix, p. 102).

Lesson Plan for a One-day Presentation

1. Pray.

2. Briefly review the material covered from the last lesson.

3. Read and discuss Chapter 12.

4. Read and carefully explain the catechism questions on p. 53.

5. Dramatize Mt 1:18—2:18.

6. Draw a picture of the Presentation.

7. Review the material covered in this class.

8. Assign Chapter 13, pp. 55—56. Make a question sheet on the content of Chapter 13 and the catechism question.

9. Pray.

Suggested Schedule for a Five-day Presentation

1. Nativity

   Aim: to tell the story of the birth of Christ.

   Activities: see activities 2, 4, and 6.

2. Flight into Egypt

   Aim: to tell the story of the visit of the Magi, the flight of the Holy Family into Egypt, and the Slaughter of the Innocents (you might want to use this story to teach respect for human life).

   Activities: see activities 1 and 4.

3. Incarnation

   Aim: to explain the doctrine of the Incarnation.

   Activities: see activities 1 and 5.

4. Incarnation

   Aim: to explain the doctrine of the Incarnation.

   Activities: see activities 1 and 5.

5. Review

   Aim: to review this week's material.

   Activities: pray or dramatize the Joyful Mysteries of the Rosary, review game, quiz.

Notes:

CHAPTER 13

The Holy Family

Background Reading for the Teacher:

Lawler, pp. 81−96. Mt 2:19−23.
Hardon, pp. 108−149. Lk 2:39−52.

Aims:

The students should be able to tell the story of the Finding in the Temple; to list the five Joyful Mysteries; to take the Holy Family as an example for their family life by accepting God's will for them, doing the job they are supposed to do in the family, making God a member of their family, and doing good for others with their family.

Materials Needed:

Bibles, map (chalkboard drawing or photocopies for each student), paper, pencils, crayons, props, old Christmas cards (or pictures of the Holy Family), construction paper, scissors, glue, glitter (optional).

Activities

1. Tell the story of St. Catherine of Siena. At one point in Catherine's life, her family was very much upset with her because she stayed in her room and prayed all day, and she refused to have any interest in getting married. Her parents dismissed most of their servants and made St. Catherine do most of the housework. In order to keep her eyes on Christ all the time that she was working, she served her father as if he were St. Joseph, her mother as if she were Mary, and her brothers and sisters as if they were the apostles.

2. Make a triptych of the Holy Family (using old Christmas cards and construction paper) for family devotions at home.

3. List the things the family might do to help others (for example, visiting a nursing home or helping to support a refugee family).

4. Draw pictures of the Holy Family, of the Finding in the Temple, or of life in the home at Nazareth.

5. Review and pray the Joyful Mysteries of the Rosary.

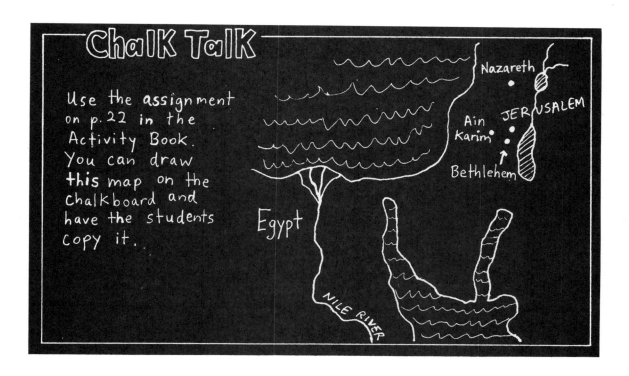

Use the assignment on p. 22 in the Activity Book. You can draw this map on the chalkboard and have the students copy it.

6. Dramatize the Joyful Mysteries.

7. Read Chapter 13 and discuss how ordinary the Holy Family's life was; yet it was lived extraordinarily well. How can our families be more like the Holy Family?

Lesson Plan for a One-day Presentation

1. Pray.

2. Review the material covered in the last lesson.

3. Read Chapter 13 and discuss how ordinary the Holy Family's life was. How can our families be more like the Holy Family?

4. Draw a map of Israel on p. 22 of the Activity Book and locate the events listed there.

5. Tell the story of St. Catherine of Siena and her family (see activity 1, above).

6. Discuss how the students can make God a member of their families.

7. Make a triptych (see activity 2).

8. Review by talking about the Joyful Mysteries. Pray them or dramatize them.

9. Assign Chapter 14, pp. 57−59.

10. Pray (if you didn't pray the Joyful Mysteries).

**Suggested Schedule for a
Five-day Presentation**

1. Finding in the Temple
   Aim: to tell the story of the Finding in the Temple.
   Activities: see activities 4 and 6.

2. Private life of Jesus
   Aim: to take the Holy Family as an example for their family life.
   Activities: see activities 4 and 7.

3. The Holy Family and your students' families
   Aim: to take the Holy Family as an example for their family life by accepting God's will for them and by doing the job they are supposed to do in the family.
   Activities: see activity 1.

4. The Holy Family and your students' families
   Aim: to take the Holy Family as an example for their family life by making God a member of their families and by doing good for others with their families.
   Activities: see activities 2 and 3.

5. Review
   Aim: to review the week's material.
   Activities: see activities 5 and 6, review game, quiz.

Notes:

CHAPTER 14

The Kingdom of Heaven

Background Reading for the Teacher:

Lawler, pp. 112−116,
   118−121.
Hardon, pp. 108−149.

Mt 3:1−4:25.
Mk 4:1−34.

Aims:

The students should be able to explain John the Baptist's role in preparing the way for Christ; to recount and explain the Baptism of Christ; to tell the story of Christ's fasting in the desert and his temptation by Satan; to define *parable* and to tell and explain some of the parables; to tell of Christ' dedication to the Father's will; and to imitate Christ's obedience in their lives. Explain that Christ's Kingdom of truth, justice, love, and peace are only fully and perfectly realized in heaven, but at the same time must be begun and worked for here on earth.

Materials Needed:

Bibles, paper, pencils, crayons, Activity Book, props.

Activities

1. Read Mt 3:1−12 and discuss John the Baptist's humility. He could have claimed to be the Messiah but he points the way to Christ instead.

2. Draw a picture of Christ's Baptism (see the picture on p. 57 in the text for ideas).

3. Read or dramatize the Temptation of Christ (Mt 4:1−11).

4. Complete the assignment on p. 23 in the Activity Book.

5. Read and explain some parables to the students (see Mk 4:1−34); have them write a parable of their own.

6. Read Jn 4:31−34 and discuss how Christ always did his Father's will even when it was very difficult. How can we be more obedient to the Father's will?

7. List ways we can be more obedient to God's will (for example, immediate and cheerful obedience to parents, respect for teachers, etc.).

8. Read and discuss St. Augustine's statement on p. 58 of the text.

Lesson Plan for a One-day Presentation

1. Pray.

2. Review the hidden life of Jesus.

3. Read Mt 3; discuss John the Baptist's humility and Jesus' Baptism.

4. Draw a picture of Jesus being baptized.

5. Complete the first part of the assignment on p. 23 of the Activity Book.

6. Read the text for a summary of Christ's teaching (pp. 57−59).

7. Read and explain some of the parables Jesus used. A parable is a simple story which uses everyday things to explain a truth. Have the children write their own modern parables using the things around them to explain God's love or the Kingdom of God (or use the second Activity Book assignment, p. 23).

8. Review material covered in this lesson.

9. Assign Chapter 15, pp. 61−63. Make question sheet on chapter content, Words to Know, and the catechism questions.

10. Pray.

Notes:

Suggested Schedule for a Five-day Presentation

1. John the Baptist
   Aim: to review the private life of Jesus; to explain John the Baptist's role in preparing the way for Christ.
   Activities: see activity 1.

2. Baptism and Temptation of the Lord
   Aim: to recount the event of the Lord's Baptism; to explain the significance of the words of the Father and the Descending of the Holy Spirit; to tell the story of Christ's fasting and Temptation and to discuss their significance.
   Activities: see activities 2, 3, and 4.

3. Teaching and parables
   Aim: to summarize briefly Christ's teachings; to define the word *parable* and explain the three parables mentioned in the text.
   Activities: see activities 4, 5, and 8.

4. Obedience to the Father's Will
   Aim: to tell of Christ's dedication to the Father's will; to imitate Christ's obedience to the Father.
   Activities: see activities 6 and 7.

5. Review
   Aim: to review the week's material.
   Activities: review game or quiz.

CHAPTER 15

The Father and I Are One

Background Reading for the Teacher:

Lawler, pp. 116−124.

Hardon, pp. 108−149.

Mt 16:13−20; 17:1−8.

Mk 1:21−45; 4:35−41; 5:1−20.

Aims:

The students should be able to demonstrate that Christ is God from the Father's testimony at his Baptism and Transfiguration, from his miracles, and from Peter's profession of faith; and to define the term *miracle*.

Materials Needed:

Bibles, paper, pencils, crayons, Activity Books.

Activities

1. Christ claimed to be God. We have three responses that we can choose: Jesus is crazy, Jesus is blaspheming, or Jesus really is who he says he is. Discuss the choices. How can we demonstrate that Jesus really is God? (By the Father's testimony, and miracles.)

2. Review the Baptism of Christ and read the account of the Transfiguration (Mt 17:1−8). Discuss how the Father's testimony in both cases shows that Jesus is truly God.

3. Read some of the Gospel accounts of Jesus' miracles. What is a miracle? How would these miracles prove that Jesus is who he says he is? (God is the only one who can work miracles. If he allows a miracle to take place at someone's intercession, it means that he approves of what that person is saying or doing. Jesus says he is God. Jesus performs miracles, which means that God approves of what Jesus is doing. Therefore, Jesus is who he says he is: God.)

4. Discuss modern-day miracles. There are three kinds of miracles: nature miracles, like Jesus' calming of the storm, or multiplying of the loaves and fish; physical miracles, like Jesus' curing people; and spiritual or moral miracles such as converts and saints. Did you know that for saints to be canonized they have to have had four miracles come about through their intercession? Explain to the children the process

by which the Church verifies true miracles. (In the case of physical cures, there must be medical evidence beforehand that the case was hopeless and medical verification afterward that there has been a sudden and permanent cure.) This discussion should help the students to see that Christ's miracles are not "fairy tales", but real, verifiable events.

5. Draw a picture of one of Christ's miracles (curing the sick, walking on water, etc.).

6. Explain and discuss the catechism questions on pp. 62—63. Have the students write a paragraph on how we know Jesus is God.

7. Dramatize Peter's profession of faith (Mt 16:13—20) and the Transfiguration (Mt 17: 1—8).

8. Use the Activity Book assignment as a review of the lesson.

Lesson Plan for a One-day Presentation

1. Pray.

2. Review Chapter 14, especially the Baptism of Christ.

3. Discuss Christ's claim to be God (see activity 1).

4. Read and discuss the Transfiguration (Mt 17:1—8). In both the Baptism and Transfiguration of Jesus, the Father witnesses to Christ: "This is my Beloved Son. Listen to him."

5. Read some of the Gospel accounts of Jesus' miracles, and tell the students about some modern miracles (see activities 3 and 4).

6. Draw a picture of one of Christ's miracles.

7. Explain the catechism questions on pp. 62—63 in the text and have the students complete the Activity Book assignment on p. 24.

8. Assign Chapter 16, pp. 64—65 for next week.

9. Pray.

Suggested Schedule for a Five-day Presentation

1. The Father's witness
   Aim: to demonstrate Christ's divinity by the testimony of his Father.
   Activities: review God's witness to Christ's divinity at his Baptism and his Transfiguration; see activities 1 and 2.

2. Miracles
   Aim: to define the term *miracle* (see Q. 55 on p. 63 in the text); to demonstrate Christ's divinity by the miracles he performed.
   Activities: see activities 3 and 4.

3. Miracles
   Aim: see day 2.
   Activities: review day 2; see activity 5.

4. Peter's profession of faith
   Aim: to tell the story of Peter's witness to Christ's divinity and the Transfiguration.
   Activities: see activities 6, 7, and 8.

5. Review
   Aim: review the week's lessons.
   Activities: review game, quiz, or see activity 8.

CHAPTER 16

Your Sins Are Forgiven

Background Reading for the Teacher:

Lawler, pp. 116−124.　　　　　　Mk 2.
Hardon, pp. 108−149.　　　　　　Lk 15.

Aims:

The students should be able to demonstrate Christ's divinity by his forgiving sins; to forgive others as God has forgiven them.

Materials Needed:

Bibles, props, paper, crayons, pencils.

Activities

1. Read and discuss Chapter 16 in class. What did the Pharisees think of Christ when he told the paralytic that his sins were forgiven him? How does the cure of the paralytic prove that Jesus can really forgive sins and, therefore, really is God?

2. Draw a picture of the cure of the paralytic (Mk 2:1−12).

3. Tell the stories of Zacchaeus (Lk 19:1−10), and Dismas (Lk 23:39−43). Tell the stories of other great sinners who became great saints (for example, St. Augustine believed in the Manichean heresy before he was baptized and became a great saint and doctor of the Church, or St. Paul, who, before he was converted, persecuted the Christians and oversaw the murder of St. Stephen. You can never judge a person as lost, be-cause God always gives everybody a chance to repent. Both Judas and Peter betrayed Jesus. Both had the opportunity to repent. One took the opportunity and he became the first Pope and a great saint.

4. Read the parables of God's mercy in Lk 15. Have the students make up a parable about God's mercy using modern day things.

5. Dramatize the parable of the prodigal son (Lk 15:11−32).

6. Read and discuss the parable of the unforgiving debtor (Mt 18:23−35). God has more reason not to forgive us than we have for not forgiving our neighbors.

7. Complete the Activity Book assignment on pp. 25−26.

Lesson Plan for a One-Day Presentation

1. Pray.

2. Review the material covered in the last lesson.

3. Read and discuss Chapter 16 in class (see activity 1).

4. Draw a picture of the cure of the paralytic.

5. Jesus used parables to show how much God wants to bring back sinners to himself. Read the parable of the prodigal son and have the students write a parable showing God's mercy (see activity 4).

6. Jesus came to call sinners to repentance. Tell the stories of some of the saints who accepted Jesus' invitation to return to the Father (see activity 3).

7. Discuss with the students how we must forgive others as we have been forgiven by God (see activity 6).

8. Review the material covered in this lesson by completing the assignment in the Activity Book, pp. 25–26.

9. Assign Chapter 17, pp. 66–67.

10. Pray.

Suggested Schedule for a Five-day Presentation

1. The cure of the paralytic
   Aim: to demonstrate Christ's divinity by his forgiving sins.
   Activities: see activities 1 and 2.

2. Parables on God's mercy
   Aim: see day 1.
   Activities: see activities 4 and 5.

3. The self-righteous vs. the repentant sinner
   Aim: to forgive others as God has forgiven us.
   Activities: see activity 3.

4. Forgive as you are forgiven
   Aim: see day 3.
   Activities: see activity 6.

5. Review
   Aim: to review the week's material.
   Activities: see activity 7, review game, quiz.

Notes:

CHAPTER 17

True God and True Man

Background Reading for the Teacher:

Lawler, pp. 81—96.
Hardon, pp. 108—149.

Aims:

The students should be able to show that Jesus is true God and true man; to see Jesus as Savior, Brother, and Model.

Materials Needed:

Bibles, paper, pencils, crayons, glue (optional), photocopies of the pattern for the paper figurine of the Sacred Heart (optional, see Appendix, p. 103), scissors (optional), Activity Book.

Activities

1. Review catechism questions 45—52 on p. 53 of the text.

2. Read and discuss Chapter 17 in class.

3. Tell the story of St. Margaret Mary and the Sacred Heart.

4. Draw a picture or make a paper figurine of the Sacred Heart (see the Appendix, p. 103).

5. Write a paragraph on St. Augustine's statement on p. 67 in the text. How is Christ the Fatherland? How is he our Way?

6. Make a poster with the message, ''What would Christ want me to do in this situation?''

7. Complete the Activity Book assignment on p. 27.

Lesson Plan for a One-day Presentation

1. Pray.

2. Review catechism questions 45—52 in the text.

3. See chalk talk to explain the doctrine of the hypostatic union.

4. Complete the assignment on p. 27 of the Activity Book.

5. Tell the story of St. Margaret Mary and

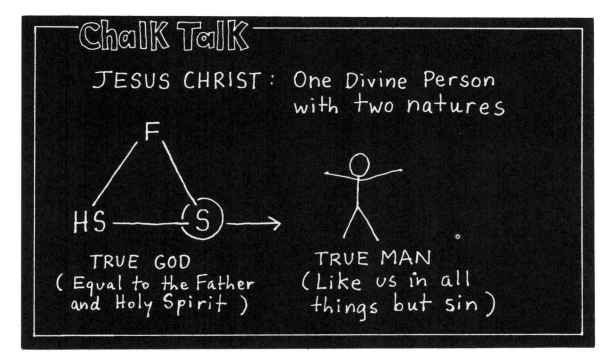

the Sacred Heart of Jesus; discuss the meaning of the Sacred Heart as the embodiment of Jesus' divine and human love for all men and women.

6. Make a paper figurine of the Sacred Heart.

7. Have the students write a paragraph on St. Augustine's statement, or make a small poster with the message, "What would Christ want me to do in this situation?" to be displayed at home.

8. Review the material covered in this lesson.

9. Assign Chapter 18, pp. 68–70. (Make up a question sheet on catechism questions 45–52.)

10. Pray.

Suggested Schedule for a Five-day Presentation

1. Jesus: true God
   Aim: to show that Jesus is true God, that is, a Divine Person.

Activities: review Chapters 15 and 16; see activities 1, 2, and chalk talk on hypostatic union.

2. Jesus: true man
   Aim: to show that Jesus is true man, that is, a Divine Person with a human body, soul, mind, and will.
   Activities: see activities 1, 2, 7, and chalk talk on hypostatic union.

3. The Sacred Heart
   Aim: to show that Jesus is true God and true man.
   Activities: see activities 3 and 4.

4. Model for mankind
   Aim: to see Jesus as Savior, Brother, and Model.
   Activities: see activities 5 and 6.

5. Review
   Aim: to review the material covered this week.
   Activities: review game, quiz, activity 7, if not used earlier in the week.

CHAPTER 18

Rejected by the Proud

Background Reading for the Teacher:

Mt 15:1−20; 19:1−12; 21:
23−46.
Mk 3:22−30.

Jn 6:44−71; 7:20−24; 9:13−41;
11:45−54.

Aims:

The students should be able to compare the expected Messiah with the real Messiah;
to tell some of the stories about the Pharisees trying to trap Jesus; to explain how
mortal and venial sin turn us away from God.

Materials Needed:

Activity Book, Bibles, pencils, paper, copies of songs.

Activities

1. Discuss the difference between the expected Messiah (a political liberator that would bring Israel into world dominance; this idea was very hard to overcome, see Acts 1:6−7) and the actual Messiah (a humble and suffering Redeemer who came to save all people from their sins, see Is 50:4−9; 52:13−53:12).

2. Complete the Activity Book assignment on p. 28.

3. Read Jn 6:44−71; have the students put themselves in the place of the apostles. Will they follow Jesus even though he says that they must eat his body and drink his blood or will they follow the crowd and leave Jesus?

4. People were very much surprised about Christ's teaching on riches. Have the students think up modern day examples of the camel going through the needle's eye. Why are riches so dangerous? How can we use our possessions to get us to heaven and not to hell?

5. Learn a song on the Eucharist, such as "I am the Bread of Life", or "Ecce Panis Angelorum" (be sure to translate the Latin hymn for the students).

6. Pretend that you are an eyewitness to the cure of the man born blind. Write a paragraph on what happened (see Jn 9:1−41).

7. Read and discuss the attempts to trap Jesus: Mt 19:1−12; Mt 22:15−46.

Chalk Talk

What is present before and after the Consecration of the bread and wine?

Before		After	
Appearance	Substance	Appearance	Substance
bread	bread	bread	Christ's Body Blood, Soul and Divinity
wine	wine	wine	

8. Discuss the last section in Chapter 18 on sin. How can we avoid mortal sin? How can we make reparation to Jesus for sins?

Lesson Plan for a One-day Presentation

1. Pray.

2. Briefly review Chapter 17.

3. Discuss the difference between the expected and the actual Messiah (see activity 1).

4. Complete the assignment on p. 28 of the Activity Book.

5. Discuss some of Jesus' teachings and how they upset the leaders of the Jewish people (see the background reading for the teacher, or activity 4).

6. Read and discuss Jn 6:44−71 (see activity 3).

7. Explain what is present before and after the Consecration of the Mass (see chalk talk chart).

8. Read and discuss the attempts to trap Jesus (activity 7).

9. The Scribes and Pharisees weren't the only ones to reject Jesus; many people throughout history have refused to love God and his Christ. Discuss mortal and venial sin with the students (see activity 8) and use the chalk talk chart on mortal and venial sin to help them understand. Be sure they know the three conditions for a sin to be mortal.

10. Review the material covered in this lesson.

11. Assign Chapter 19, pp. 71−74.

12. Pray.

Suggested Schedule for a Five-day Presentation

1. The expected vs. the real Messiah
   Aim: to compare the expectations of the people with Jesus' real mission.
   Activities: see activities 1 and 2.

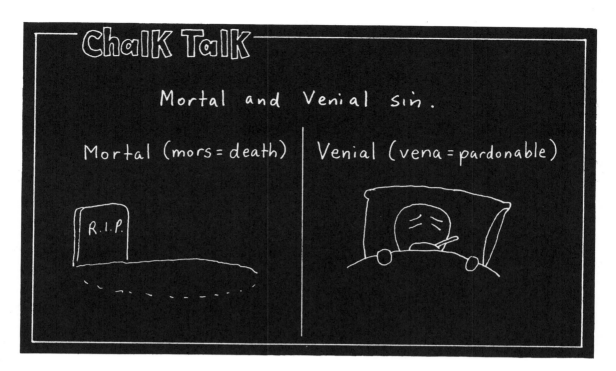

2. Hard teachings
   Aim: to explain Jesus' teaching on riches and curing on the Sabbath; his prophecies of the Eucharist.
   Activities: see activities 3, 4, 5, and chalkboard chart on the Consecration.

3. Attempts to trap Jesus
   Aim: to tell some of the stories about the leaders of the people trying to trap Jesus.
   Activities: see activities 6 and 7.

4. Turning away from Christ
   Aim: to explain how mortal and venial sin turn us away from God.
   Activities: see activity 8 and chalk talk on sin.

5. Review
   Aim: to review this week's material.
   Activities: review game, quiz.

Notes:

CHAPTER 19

The Acceptance of the Father's Will

Background Reading for the Teacher:

Lawler, pp. 125−131.   Jn 11:1−44; 12:1−19.
Mt 21:1−11.

Aims:

The students should be able to describe the events of the last week of Christ's life; to appreciate all the suffering that Christ underwent for our salvation.

Materials Needed:

Bibles, songs (optional), thorn branches (optional), big nails or spikes (optional), missalettes (optional), props (optional), pictures of the Shroud of Turin (in text or in *National Geographic*'s June 1980 issue), paper, pencil, crayons (optional), butcher paper (optional).

Activities

1. Dramatize the Palm Sunday procession (Jn 12:12−19).

2. Sing "All Glory, Laud, and Honor".

3. Read and discuss Jn 10 about Jesus, the Good Shepherd.

4. Sing "Shepherd of Souls".

5. Act out the Mass using missalettes.

6. Enact a Passover Meal (see Chapter 8, Activity 5 and "Materials Needed").

7. Look at the pictures of the Shroud of Turin and explain the physical sufferings of Christ from the Agony in the Garden to the death on the Cross.

8. Show a thorn branch or make a "crown of thorns" to help the students appreciate Jesus' sufferings.

9. Have the students meditate on the Passion of Jesus for a few minutes and then write a prayer to Jesus thanking him for what he did for them and telling him what they will do for him to return such a great amount of love.

10. Read and discuss Jn 19:25−27: Jesus giving his Mother to Saint John and to us, and giving us to Mary.

11. Dramatize the Sorrowful Mysteries of the Rosary.

Suggested Schedule for a Five-day Presentation

1. Palm Sunday / the Good Shepherd
   Aim: to describe the events of the last week of Christ's life; to explain that Jesus, the Good Shepherd, *laid down* his life for his sheep.
   Activities: see activities 1–4.

2. The Last Supper
   Aim: to describe the events of the last week of Christ's life.
   Activities: see activities 5 and 6; read and discuss Jn 13:1–20.

3. The Passion of the Lord
   Aim: to describe the events of the last week of Christ's earthly life; to appreciate all the sufferings that Jesus underwent for our salvation.
   Activities: see activities 7–9.

4. The Sorrowful Mother
   Aim: to show Mary's role in the Redemption.
   Activities: see activities 10 and 11.

5. Review
   Aim: to review this week's material.
   Activities: review game, quiz; make a mural of the Passion of Christ.

Lesson Plan for a One-day Presentation

1. Pray.

2. Briefly review Chapter 18.

3. Tell the story of the entrance of Jesus into Jerusalem on Palm Sunday (Jn 12:12–19).

4. Read the account of the Last Supper (Jn 13:1–20) and discuss Christ's humility in washing the feet of his disciples. How can we imitate Christ's humility?

5. Show the "crown of thorns" to the students; talk about Christ's physical sufferings (see activities 7 and 8).

6. Dramatize the Sorrowful Mysteries of the Rosary.

7. Read and discuss Jn 19:25–27 (see activity 10).

8. Meditate on the Passion (see activity 9).

9. Assign Chapter 20, pp. 75–77.

10. Pray.

Notes:

CHAPTER 20

The Perfect Sacrifice

Background Reading for the Teacher:

Lawler, pp. 125−136.　　　　　　　Lk 21:1−4.
Hardon, pp. 465−481.

Aims:

The students should be able to define the word *sacrifice*; to explain how the only sacrifice that can gain grace for mankind is the sacrifice of Christ; to list ways they can offer sacrifices in union with Christ's sacrifice; to explain how the sacrifice of Christ is continued in the sacrifice of the Mass; to understand better the true value of the Mass.

Materials Needed:

Paper, pencils, crayons, butcher paper (optional), Activity Book, Bibles.

Activities

1. Draw pictures of sacrifices in the Old Testament (as a mural or a book): Cain and Abel's sacrifice, Melchizedek's sacrifice, Abraham's sacrifice of Isaac, the Israelite's sacrifice (Lev 1:3−9). Draw a picture of Christ's sacrifice.

2. Complete the Activity Book assignment on pp. 31−32.

3. List things that we can do to share in Christ's sacrifice (for example, not eating candy, giving up a favorite TV program, taking time to visit the elderly, doing homework without complaining).

4. Read this poem:
   Limbo

   The ancient greyness shifted
   Suddenly and thinned
   Like mist upon the moors
   Before the wind.
   An old, old prophet lifted
   A shining face and said:
   "He will be coming soon.
   The Son of God is dead;
   He died this afternoon."

   A murmurous excitement stirred
   All souls.

They wondered if they dreamed—
Save one old man who seemed
Not even to have heard.

And Moses standing,
Hushed them all to ask
If any had a welcome song prepared.
If not, would David take the task?
And if they cared
Could not the three young children sing
The Benedicite, the canticle of praise
They made when God kept them from per-
    ishing
In the fiery blaze?

A breath of spring surprised them,
Stilling Moses' words.
No one could speak, remembering
The first fresh flowers,
The little singing birds.
Still others thought of fields new ploughed
Or apple trees
All blossom-boughed.
Or some, the way a dried bed fills
With water
Laughing down green hills.
The fisherfolk dreamed of the foam
On bright blue seas.
The one old man who had not stirred
Remembered home.

And there He was
Splendid as the morning sun and fair
As only God is fair.
And they, confused with joy,
Knelt to adore
Seeing that He wore
Five crimson stars
He never had before.

No canticle at all was sung.
None toned a psalm, or raised a greeting
    song.
A silent man alone
Of all that throng
Found tongue—
Not any other.

Close to His heart
When the embrace was done,
Old Joseph said,
"How is Your Mother,
How is Your Mother, Son?"[1]

5. Jesus saved those who died both before and after his death on the Cross. Those who died before the Resurrection waited in "hell". Explain the term "He descended into hell". In this instance, hell means the place where the souls of the just who died before Christ's Resurrection awaited their salvation. Jesus descended into hell to bring their souls with him to God. They included Moses, Abel, Abraham, Melchizedek, and many other just souls. Explain why Jesus can be the Savior of all time, not just of people who lived *after* his Incarnation.

6. Explain how Christ's sacrifice is the only sacrifice that could make up for our sins. Use the following analogy: If the Queen of England, while visiting the United States, were hit in the face with a pie by an American citizen, what would have to be done to make up for the insult? Would it do if only the pie-throwing citizen apologized, or would it be necessary for the President to apologize also? The greater the dignity of the person offended, the greater the offense. Someone of equal dignity to the person offended and yet one with the person who offended would have to make up for the offense. In the case of sin, God who is of infinite dignity is, therefore, infinitely offended by sin. Mankind needs a redeemer who is equal to God in dignity and yet a man too. Only Jesus is both true God and true man; only his sacrifice can make up for our sins.

[1] Sister Mary Ada, *The Mary Book* (New York: Sheed and Ward, Inc., 1950), p. 181—183.

Chalk Talk

SACRIFICE

To give up something we like | To put up with something we don't like

CANDY | POP | MATH ENGLISH HOMEWORK | PAIN

To show our love for God / to show sorrow for our sins / to thank God

7. Tell the story of St. Edmund Campion, or Blessed Kateri Tekakwitha, or the story of the Romanian priest found murdered in 1984. He had been caught saying Mass and had had bread stuffed down his throat until he was unable to breathe. Other priests and lay people in the Communist countries still risk their lives to offer or attend Mass (cf. *With God in Russia* by Rev. Walter Cizek, S.J.).

Lesson Plan for a One-day Presentation

1. Pray.

2. Briefly review Chapter 19.

3. Define the word *sacrifice* and talk about the three reasons for sacrifice; use chalk talk on sacrifice.

4. Have the children list ways they can make sacrifices in union with Jesus' sacrifice (see activity 3).

5. Complete the first part of the Activity Book assignment.

6. Have the students make a mural of the sacrifices mentioned in the Activity Book assignment and the sacrifice of the New Testament, the Crucifixion.

7. Explain how Christ's sacrifice is the only sacrifice that could make up for our sins (see activity 6).

8. By his sacrifice Christ gained grace for all people before and after his death. Read the poem *Limbo* (see activities 4 and 5).

9. Christ's sacrifice is continued for us in the Mass. Discuss the relationship between the sacrifice of the Cross and the sacrifice of the Mass using chalk talk on sacrifice; have the students fill in the chart in the second part of the Activity Book assignment.

10. Tell the students stories that will help

Chalk Talk

	SACRIFICE OF THE CROSS	SACRIFICE OF THE MASS
PRIEST	JESUS	JESUS
VICTIM	JESUS	JESUS
PURPOSE	REDEMPTION OF THE WORLD	REDEMPTION OF THE WORLD
EFFECT	REDEMPTION WAS MERITED	REDEMPTION IS COMMUNICATED
MANNER OF OFFERING	BLOODY (JESUS PAYS ENTIRE COST)	UNBLOODY (COST SHARED WITH US)

them to understand how important the Mass is to true followers of Christ (see activity 7).

11. Review the material covered in this lesson. (Don't forget to cover catechism question 58.)

12. Assign Chapter 21, pp. 78—81.

13. Pray.

Suggested Schedule for a Five-day Presentation

1. Sacrifice in the Old Testament
   Aim: to define the word *sacrifice*; to explain how the only sacrifice that can gain grace for mankind or forgiveness for man's sins is the sacrifice of Christ; to list ways we can offer sacrifice in union with Christ.
   Activities: see chalk talk on sacrifice and activities 1, 2, and 3.

2. Christ's sacrifice
   Aim: see day 1.
   Activities: see activities 1 and 6.

3. "He descended into hell"
   Aim: to show the effects of Christ's sacrifice, for those who lived before or after his sacrifice.
   Activities: see activities 4 and 5; discuss how Christ's sacrifice is made effective in our lives through the sacraments, especially baptism and the Mass.

4. The sacrifice continued
   Aim: to explain how the sacrifice of Christ is continued in the Mass; to understand better the true value of the Mass. People who understand its value are even willing to risk their lives to offer or to attend Mass.
   Activities: see activities 2, 7, and the chalk talk on the Mass.

5. Review
   Aim: see days 1—4, to review the material covered this week.
   Activities: review game, quiz.

CHAPTER 21

He Is Risen

Background Reading for the Teacher:

Lawler, pp. 137–147.
1 Cor 15:1–34.

Hardon, pp. 38, 145–146,
207–208.

Aims:

The students should be able to tell the Gospel story of Jesus' Resurrection; to explain that the Resurrection is a central truth of our faith; to show the effects of the Resurrection for Christ and for us.

Materials Needed:

Bibles, props, filmstrip (optional), Activity Book.

Activities

1. Read and discuss Chapter 21 in class (or the accounts of the Resurrection in the Gospels: Mt 28; Mk 16; Lk 24; Jn 20).

2. Dramatize the Resurrection, using the first part of the chapter or the Gospels.

3. Read and discuss 1 Cor 15:1–34. How is the Resurrection the basis for our faith? How does the Resurrection prove that Jesus is truly God? Discuss the catechism questions on p. 79.

4. Show a filmstrip on the Resurrection.

5. Complete Activity Book assignment on p. 33.

6. Go through the Easter Vigil liturgy and/or the rite of baptism. (These rites are a good way to review the history of salvation from Adam to Christ; see especially the readings for the Easter Vigil Mass.)

7. Renew your baptismal vows.

Lesson Plan for a One-day Presentation

1. Pray.

2. Review Chapter 20.

3. Read or dramatize the Resurrection (see activities 1, 2, or 5).

4. Read and discuss 1 Cor 15:1−34 (see activity 3).

5. Complete the Activity Book assignment on p. 33. Discuss the different symbols of the Resurrection. Have the students write them in the space provided.

6. Discuss what we learn of God through the Easter Vigil Mass; discuss how baptism lets us share in Jesus' death and Resurrection.

7. Review today's lesson.

8. Assign Chapter 22, pp. 82−84.

9. Pray.

Suggested Schedule for a Five-day Presentation

1. Easter Sunday
   Aim: to relate the events of the day Christ rose from the dead.

   Activities: see activities 1 and 2.

2. Easter Sunday
   Aim: see day 1
   Activities: see activity 4.

3. The Resurrection
   Aim: to explain why the Resurrection is a central truth of our faith; to show the effects of the Resurrection for us.
   Activities: see activities 3 and 5.

4. Easter Vigil
   Aim: to show the effects of the Resurrection for us.
   Activities: see activity 6 and 7.

5. Review
   Aim: to review the week's material.
   Activities: review games, quiz.

Notes:

CHAPTER 22

Jesus Sends the Apostles

Background Reading for the Teacher:

Lawler, pp. 148—149.
Jn 20—21.

Aims:

The students should be able to tell the stories of doubting Thomas, the conferral of the power to forgive sins, and Peter's primacy (Jn 21); to recount the story of Jesus' Ascension into heaven; to recognize Christ in others.

Materials Needed:

Bibles, paper (optional), crayons (optional), props (optional), Activity Book.

Activities

1. Read and discuss Jn 20:19—29; Jn 21. What power does Jesus give to the apostles? What special mission is given to Peter?

2. Complete the Activity Book assignment on pp. 34—35.

3. Draw or dramatize the story of doubting Thomas (Jn 20:24—29). How does he help us to believe in the Resurrection? What did Jesus have to say about those who have not seen the Risen Christ and still believe in him?

4. Read and discuss the account of what happened on the way to Emmaus (Lk 24:13—35). When did the disciples recognize Jesus? Can we meet Jesus today? (Yes, above all, in the Eucharist, but also in those around us.)

5. Tell the story of St. Martin of Tours (p. 84 in text) or the story of St. Catherine of Siena and the beggar who was very particular and rude about the clothes she gave him, but when Christ appeared to her that night, he told her that he was so pleased with her patience and generosity, because he had been the beggar in disguise.

6. List ways that you can see Christ in others.

7. Dramatize or draw a picture of the Ascension.

Lesson Plan for a One-day Presentation

1. Pray.

2. Read and discuss Jn 20:19—29; Jn 21 (see activity 1).

3. Draw or dramatize the story of doubting Thomas (see activity 3).

4. Dramatize or draw the Ascension.

5. Tell the stories of St. Martin and St. Catherine; have the students list ways they can recognize and love Jesus in others.

6. Complete the Activity Book assignment.

7. Review Chapters 11−22.

8. Give a test over Chapters 11−22. (You may wish to devote a whole class to review and testing.)

9. Assign Chapter 23, pp. 87−89.

10. Pray.

Suggested Schedule for a Five-day Presentation

1. Thomas' doubt
   Aim: to tell the story of doubting Thomas and explain how his doubt helps our faith; to tell the stories of the conferral of the power to forgive sins, and Peter's primacy.
   Activities: see activities 1, 2, and 3.

2. The Ascension
   Aim: to recount the story of Jesus' Ascension into heaven.
   Activities: see activities 2 and 7.

3. Recognizing Christ in others
   Aim: to recognize Christ in others.
   Activities: see activities 4, 5, and 6.

4. Review
   Aim: to review Chapters 11−22.
   Activities: review games and serious review of the material covered in Chapters 11−22.

5. Review
   Aim: see day 4.
   Activities: test on Chapters 11−22. You may wish to devote an entire week to review and testing.

Notes:

PART THREE

God the Holy Spirit, The Sanctifier

CHAPTER 23

The Giver of Life

Background Reading for the Teacher

Lawler, pp. 150–161.
Lk 24:49.

Hardon, pp. 185–189, 200–205.
Acts 1 and 2.

Aims:

The students should be able to recount the events from Christ's Ascension to Pentecost; to explain the history of Pentecost; to appreciate and understand the Holy Spirit's activities in their lives and in the life of the Church; and to list the gifts of the Holy Spirit.

Materials Needed:

Bibles, Activity Book, paper, crayons, pencils.

Activities

1. Read and discuss or dramatize Acts 2:1–47.

2. Draw a picture of the first Pentecost (see Acts 2:1–13).

3. Show a filmstrip or film on Pentecost or the Glorious Mysteries of the Rosary.

4. Complete the Activity Book assignment on pp. 36–37.

5. Sing a song to the Holy Spirit (for example, "Come Holy Ghost").

6. Have a contest to see how many references to the Holy Spirit can be found in the Gospels or Acts of the Apostles.

7. Read and discuss "God Sends His Spirit" on pp. 88–89 in the text; have the children list ways the Holy Spirit guides them in their daily lives. How can they be more attentive and obedient to him?

8. Discuss the Holy Spirit's activities in the Church; have them list some of these activities.

Lesson Plan for a One-day Presentation

1. Pray.

2. Review Chapters 18–22.

3. Read and discuss or dramatize Acts 2:1–47.

4. Draw a picture of the First Pentecost.

5. Chalk talk on the Holy Spirit.

Chalk Talk

The Holy Spirit as the Love between the Father and Son.

HS

Love for the Son

Love for the Father

F ⟶ S

6. Sing a song to the Holy Spirit.

7. Complete the Activity Book assignment on pp. 36−37.

8. Read and discuss "God Sends His Spirit" on pp. 88−89 in the text (see activities 7 and 8).

9. Review Chapter 23.

10. Assign Chapter 24, pp. 90−92. Make a question sheet on the Words to Know and the catechism questions.

11. Pray.

Suggested Schedule for a Five-day Presentation

1. Pentecost
   Aim: to recount the events from Christ's Ascension to Pentecost; to explain the history of Pentecost.
   Activities: see activities 1, 2, and 3.

2. The Holy Spirit
   Aim: to explain who the Holy Spirit is.

   Activities: see activities 4, 6, and chalk talk on the Holy Spirit.

3. The Holy Spirit in your life
   Aim: to appreciate and understand the Holy Spirit's action in your daily life.
   Activities: see activities 5 and 7; discuss baptism and confirmation, and list, define, and briefly explain the gifts of the Holy Spirit.

4. The Holy Spirit in the Church
   Aim: to explain the Holy Spirit's activities in the Church, especially in papal infallibility, the apostolate of the Church, and the universal call to sanctity. (These topics will be covered more thoroughly in later chapters.)
   Activities: see activity 8 ; read and discuss the section of the Credo of the People of God on p. 89 in the text, and the Words to Know.

5. Review
   Aim: to review this week's material.
   Activities: review game, quiz.

CHAPTER 24

The Mystical Body

Background Reading for the Teacher:

Hardon, pp. 110, 206–207, 210–211, 505.

Lawler, pp. 182–184.

Aims:

The students should be able to tell the story of Christ calling the apostles; to explain the doctrines of the Mystical Body of Christ and the Communion of Saints.

Materials Needed:

Poster board (optional), crayons or magic markers, props, paper, Activity Book.

Activities

1. Complete the Activity Book assignment on p. 38.

2. Dramatize the call of the apostles (see Mt 5:18–22; Mk 2:13–14; Jn 1:35–51; Mk 3:13–19).

3. Read and discuss the quote from 1 Cor 12 (p. 91 in the text).

4. Draw pictures of the Church Militant (the members of the Church on earth), the Church Suffering (the poor souls in purgatory), and the Church Triumphant (the saints in heaven).

5. Discuss and give a drill on the catechism questions on p. 92.

6. The Mystical Body has many members. List some of those members and their functions within the Body (for example, the Pope, bishops, priests, religious, laymen and women, missionaries, catechists, students, children).

Lesson Plan for a One-day Presentation

1. Pray.

2. Briefly review Chapter 23.

3. Dramatize the call of the apostles (see activity 2).

4. Complete the Activity Book assignment on p. 38.

5. Read and discuss the quote from 1 Cor 12 on p. 21 in the text.

6. List some of the members of the Mystical Body and their place in the Church (see activity 6).

7. Chalk talk on Church Militant, Suffering, and Triumphant.

8. Draw pictures of the Church Militant, Suffering, and Triumphant.

9. Review Chapter 24 (see activity 5).

10. Assign Chapter 25, pp. 93−95; make a question sheet on the catechism questions.

11. Pray.

Suggested Schedule for a Five-day Presentation

1. Founding of the Church
   Aim: to tell the story of Christ's calling of the apostles.
   Activities: see activities 1 and 2.

2. The Mystical Body
   Aim: to explain the doctrine of the Mystical Body of Christ.
   Activities: see activities 3 and 6.

3. The True Church
   Aim: to show that Christ is the founder of the True Church, the Catholic Church.
   Activities: see chalk talk on the major Christian churches. You might want to begin activity 4 on the Communion of Saints at this time.

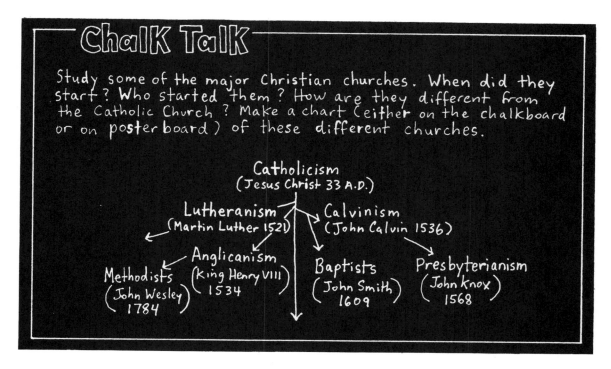

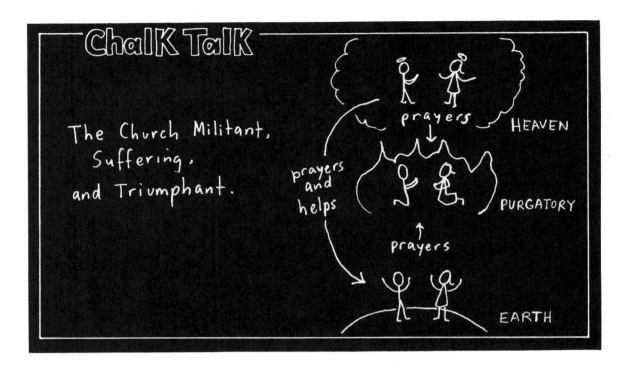

4. The Communion of Saints
   Aim: to explain the doctrine of the Communion of Saints
   Activities: see activity 4 and the chalk talk on the Church Triumphant, Suffering, and Militant.

5. Review
   Aim: to review this week's material.
   Activities: see activity 5; review games, quiz.

Notes:

CHAPTER 25

The Identity of the Church

Background Reading for the Teacher:

Lawler, pp. 178–188.
Hardon, pp. 208–223.

Aims:

The students should be able to list and explain the four marks of the Church; and to describe and explain some of the symbols of the Church.

Materials Needed:

Activity Book, resources for short reports (encyclopedias, articles—optional), paper, pencils, crayons, chart or list of popes from Peter to the present Pope (optional), Bibles.

Activities

1. Read and discuss Chapter 25 in class.

2. Discuss and give a drill on the Words to Know and the catechism questions on p. 95 in the text (flash cards or game).

3. Complete the Activity Book assignment on p. 39.

4. Have students give reports on the Church in various countries or on one of the Eastern rites of the Church.

5. Draw a picture of your favorite symbol of the Church.

6. Show a list or chart of the unbroken line of the papacy from Peter to the present Pope.

7. Pray the prayer for Church unity on p. 94 in the text.

Lesson Plan for a One-day Presentation

1. Pray.

2. Review Chapter 24, especially the section on "The True Church". (You may wish to show the chart of the Christian churches, from chalk talk in Chapter 24.) How can you tell which Church is the right Church? (the four marks of the Church).

3. Read "Four Marks", pp. 93–94 in the

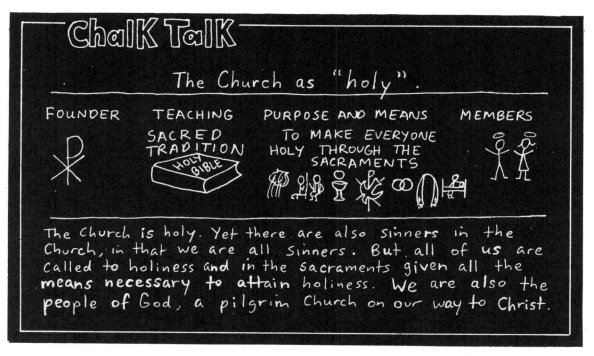

Chalk Talk

The Church as "holy".

FOUNDER　　TEACHING　　PURPOSE AND MEANS　　MEMBERS

SACRED TRADITION

HOLY BIBLE

TO MAKE EVERYONE HOLY THROUGH THE SACRAMENTS

The Church is holy. Yet there are also sinners in the Church, in that we are all sinners. But all of us are called to holiness and in the sacraments given all the means necessary to attain holiness. We are also the people of God, a pilgrim Church on our way to Christ.

text. Complete the Activity Book assignment on p. 39.

4. Draw a picture of your favorite symbol of the Church.

5. Discuss and give a drill on the catechism questions and Words to Know, on p. 95 in the text.

6. Assign Chapter 26, pp. 96–98.

Suggested Schedule for a Five-day Presentation

1. Four marks of the Church
   Aim: to list and explain the four marks of the Church.
   Activities: review the chart on the Christian churches, from chalk talk Chapter 24; see activities 1 and 3, begin activity 4.

2. One, catholic Church
   Aim: to explain the marks of the Church: *one* and *catholic*.
   Activities: see activity 4.

3. Holy, apostolic Church
   Aim: to explain the marks of the Church: *holy* and *apostolic*.
   Activities: see activity 6 and chalk talk on the Church as *holy*.

4. Symbols of the Church
   Aim: to describe and explain some of the symbols of the Church.
   Activities: see activities 3 and 5.

5. Review
   Aim: to review this week's material.
   Activities: see activity 2; review game, quiz.

CHAPTER 26

The Church Rules

Background Reading for the Teacher:

Lawler, pp. 188—196,
219—220.
Hardon, pp. 520—531.

Mt 16:18—19.
Acts 6:1—7; 15:1—35.

Aims:

The students should be able to recount some of the events in the Acts of the Apostles which show the apostles as leaders of the Church; to explain that the bishops are the successors of the apostles and, therefore, inherit the apostles' mission to rule, to teach, and to sanctify; to list and explain the hierarchy of the Church; to list the six precepts of the Church; to distinguish between those things that are changeable and unchangeable in the Church.

Materials Needed:

Bibles, butcher paper or newsprint (optional), paper, pencils, crayons, Activity Book, chart of the churches (chalk talk in Chapter 24).

Activities

1. Read and discuss Mt 16:18—19; Acts 6:1—7; 15:1—35. What power did Jesus give to the apostles? Who is in charge of determining the solutions to the problems of the early Church? Who are the successors of the apostles?

2. Make a mural of ways to obey the six precepts of the Church.

3. Explain the changeable and unchangeable aspects of the Church. Have the students write a paragraph explaining this distinction to see if they have it clear in their minds.

4. Complete the Activity Book assignment on pp. 40—41 (a good idea for a quiz).

Lesson Plan for a One-day Presentation

1. Pray.

2. Review Chapter 25.

3. Read and discuss Scripture quotes on the apostles' mission to rule (see activity 1).

4. Chalk talk on the hierarchy of the Church.

Chalk Talk

HIERARCHY OF THE CHURCH

POPE	(ARCH)BISHOPS	PRIESTS	DEACONS
PETER'S SUCCESSOR	APOSTLES' SUCCESSORS	BISHOP'S HELPER	PRIEST'S HELPER
THE CHURCH	A DIOCESE OR ARCHDIOCESE	A PARISH	A PARISH
INFALLIBLE BECAUSE OF HIS OFFICE AS POPE	INFALLIBLE IN UNION WITH THE POPE	PREACH AND TEACH IN UNION WITH HIS BISHOP	PREACH AND TEACH IN UNION WITH HIS BISHOP
MINISTERS ALL THE SACRAMENTS	MINISTERS ALL THE SACRAMENTS	ALL THE SACRAMENTS EXCEPT HOLY ORDERS	PROCLAIM THE GOSPEL, BAPTISM, MATRIMONY, FUNERALS, DISTRIBUTES HOLY COMMUNION

5. Have the students draw a mural of ways to obey the six precepts of the Church.

6. Explain what can change and what cannot change in the Church (see activity 3).

7. Complete the Activity Book assignment on pp. 40–41.

8. Review the material covered in this lesson.

9. Assign Chapter 27, pp. 99–101.

10. Pray.

Suggested Schedule for a Five-day Presentation

1. The apostles' mission
   Aim: to recount some of the events in the Acts of the Apostles which show the apostles as leaders of the Church.
   Activities: see activity 1.

2. Hierarchy of the Church
   Aim: to explain that the bishops are the successors of the apostles and, therefore, inherit the apostles' mission to rule the Church; to list and explain the hierarchy of the Church.
   Activities: see chalk talk on the hierarchy of the Church.

3. Precepts of the Church
   Aim: to list the six precepts of the Church.
   Activities: see activity 2.

4. Aspects of the Church
   Aim: to distinguish between those things that are changeable and those that are unchangeable in the Church.
   Activities: see activity 3.

5. Review
   Aim: to review the material for this week.
   Activities: see activity 4; review game and / or quiz.

CHAPTER 27

Teach All Nations

Background Reading for the Teacher:

Lawler, pp. 199–219.   Jn 14:26; 16:13.
Hardon, pp. 224–233.

Aims:

The students should be able to define *Sacred Tradition*, *Sacred Scripture* and *Magisterium*, and to explain their interrelatedness; to explain the doctrine of infallibility; to explain the Church's mission to evangelize all nations.

Materials Needed:

Chart of the churches from Chapter 24, Activity Book, paper, pencils.

Activities

1. Play "telephone" to demonstrate what happens when there is no one to check back to keep a message the same (see text, p. 99 for how to play).

2. Refer back to the chart of the churches (in Chapter 24). In the United States, there are over 265 different Protestant denominations.[1] Why do Protestants keep splitting into more and more groups? (Because they don't have a teaching authority, a Magisterium, to guide them.)

3. Complete the Activity Book assignment on p. 42.

4. Have the students list ways they can help in the Church's mission of spreading the gospel.

5. Discuss and give a drill on the Words to Know and the catechism questions.

6. Have the students memorize this quote from *Dei Verbum* #10: "Sacred Tradition, Sacred Scripture, and the Magisterium of the Church are so connected and associated that one cannot stand without the others."

Lesson Plan for a One-day Presentation

1. Pray.

2. Review Chapter 26.

---

[1] William Whalen, *Separated Brethren* (Huntington: Our Sunday Visitor, 1979), p. 11.

Chalk Talk

The unity of Sacred Tradition, Sacred Scripture, and the teaching authority of the Church.

TRADITION

Tradition is safeguarded by the Magisterium, and the Magisterium gets its teaching from Tradition.

Tradition contains the list of the books of Scripture and Scripture's interpretation.

MAGISTERIUM ←→ SCRIPTURE

The Magisterium gets what to teach from Scripture, and Scripture can only be authentically interpreted by the Magisterium.

3. Demonstrate the need for the teaching authority of the Church (see activities 1 and 2).

4. Complete the Activity Book assignment on p. 42.

5. Have the students list ways they can participate in the Church's mission.

6. Discuss the interrelationship among Sacred Tradition, Sacred Scripture, and the Magisterium of the Church (see activity 6 and chalk talk).

7. Discuss and give a drill on the Words to Know and the catechism questions.

8. Assign Chapter 28, pp. 102−108.

9. Pray.

Suggested Schedule for a Five-day Presentation

1. Tradition, Scripture, and Magisterium
   Aim: to define *Sacred Tradition, Sacred Scripture,* and *Magisterium* and to explain their interrelatedness.
   Activities: see activities 1 and 2.

2. Tradition, Scripture, and Magisterium
   Aim: see day 1.
   Activities: see activity 6 and chalk talk.

3. Magisterium
   Aim: see day 1; to explain the doctrine of infallibility.
   Activities: see activity 5; read and discuss Chapter 27, especially on papal infallibility.

4. Evangelization
   Aim: to explain the Church's mission to evangelize all nations.
   Activities: see activities 3 and 4.

5. Review
   Aim: to review this week's material.
   Activities: review game, quiz.

CHAPTER 28

Called to Holiness

Background Reading for the Teacher:

Lawler, pp. 220−221,
   253−262, 292−296.

Hardon, pp. 419−437,
   457−520.

Aims:

The students should be able to make an analogy between their physical life as children of their parents and their spiritual life as children of God; to define the word *sacrament* and to list the seven sacraments; to explain the sacraments of baptism, penance, Eucharist and confirmation; to define *actual sin*, *mortal sin*, and *venial sin*; to list the three things that make a sin mortal and the five things necessary for a good confession.

Materials Needed:

Activity Book, paper, pencils, crayons.

Activities

1. Read and discuss Chapter 28 in class.

2. Define *sacrament* and discuss how the sacraments are different than the signs children normally see. Why did Jesus institute the sacraments?

3. Review the doctrine on original sin and explain actual sin, mortal sin, and venial sin. Have the students memorize the three things that make a sin mortal (use the example on p. 103 in the text).

4. Write on the board the five steps for a good confession; have the students memorize them. Be sure they know the Act of Contrition (see p. 127 in the text).

5. Complete the Activity Book assignment on p. 43.

6. Discuss and give a drill on the catechism questions and Words to Know.

Chalk Talk

Have the students make a chart on baptism, penance, Communion, and confirmation, making an analogy between natural and supernatural life.

NATURAL	SUPERNATURAL
BIRTH	BAPTISM
MEDICINE	PENANCE
FOOD	COMMUNION
ADULTHOOD	CONFIRMATION

Lesson Plan for a One-day Presentation

1. Pray.

2. Review Chapter 27 and original sin (Chapter 6).

3. Define the word *sacrament* and discuss (see activity 2).

4. Make a chart on baptism, penance, Communion, and confirmation. How are these sacraments related to our spiritual life? (See chalk talk.)

5. Ask the students to define actual, mortal, and venial sin. What are the three things that make a sin mortal?

6. Have the students memorize the five things needed for a good confession (see activity 4).

7. Complete the Activity Book assignment on p. 43.

8. Discuss and give a drill on the catechism questions and the Words to Know on pp. 105−108.

9. Assign Chapter 29, pp. 109−112.

10. Pray.

Suggested Schedule for a Five-day Presentation

1. Children of God
   Aim: to make an analogy between the students' physical life as children of their parents and their spiritual life as children of God.
   Activities: see activity 1.

2. The sacraments
   Aim: to define the word *sacrament* and to list the seven sacraments; to explain the

sacraments of baptism, penance, Eucharist, and confirmation.

Activities: see activity 2 and chalk talk.

3. Baptism and penance

   Aim: to explain the sacraments of baptism and penance.

   Activities: review original sin. What are the effects of baptism on the soul? Why are some of the effects of original sin not removed? Why do we need confession? (See activities 4 and 5.)

4. Sin

   Aim: to define *actual sin*, *mortal sin*, and *venial sin*; to list the three things that make a sin mortal and the five things necessary for a good confession.

   Activities: see activities 3 and 6.

5. Review

   Aim: to review this week's material.

   Activities: see activity 6; review game or quiz.

Notes:

CHAPTER 29

The Mother of God in Our Lives

Background Reading for the Teacher:

Lawler, pp. 222–234.   Jn 2:1–2; 19:25–27.
Hardon, pp. 150–171.

Aims:

The students should be able to tell the stories of Mary's intercession in the Bible; to explain the dogma of her Assumption into heaven; to know how to pray the Rosary and the Mysteries of the Rosary; to tell the story of at least one of the apparitions of Mary.

Materials Needed:

Filmstrip (optional), props (optional), Bibles, Activity Book, rosaries, paper, crayons.

Activities

1. Dramatize or draw the wedding feast at Cana (Jn 2:1–12); discuss Mary's role as intercessor.

2. Complete the Activity Book assignment on pp. 44–45. See pp. 121–123 in the text for dates and explanations. (Feast of the Immaculate Heart of Mary on the Saturday after the Feast of the Sacred Heart; Our Lady of Guadalupe, December 12; Our Lady of Lourdes, February 11; Our Lady of Mt. Carmel, July 16; Our Lady of the Rosary [commemorating the victory of Lepanto], October 7.)

3. Learn the *Hail Holy Queen*; see p. 111 in the text.

4. Draw a picture of Mary's Assumption into heaven.

5. Pray or dramatize the Glorious Mysteries of the Rosary.

6. Show a filmstrip on Our Lady of Guadalupe, Lourdes, or Fatima, or tell the stories.

7. Sing "Immaculate Mary" (Lourdes hymn).

8. Review how to say the Rosary.

Lesson Plan for a One-day Presentation

1. Pray.

2. Review Chapter 28.

3. Read and dramatize or draw the wedding feast at Cana (see activity 1).

4. Tell the students about the dogma of the Assumption of Mary. Have them draw a picture of the Assumption.

5. Review how to say the Rosary. Pray or dramatize the Five Glorious Mysteries. Learn the *Hail Holy Queen*.

6. Show a filmstrip or video on an apparition of Mary (see activity 6).

7. Complete the Activity Book assignment.

8. Review the material covered in this lesson.

9. Assign Chapter 30, pp. 113–117.

10. Pray.

Suggested Schedule for a Five-day Presentation

1. Mary in the Bible
   Aim: to tell the Bible stories of Mary's intercession.
   Activities: see activity 1; discuss Jn 19: 25–27.

2. The Assumption
   Aim: to explain the dogma of Mary's Assumption into heaven.
   Activities: see activity 4; review and discuss original sin and Mary's Immaculate Conception.

3. The Rosary
   Aim: to know how to pray the Rosary and the Mysteries of the Rosary.
   Activities: see activities 3, 5, and 8.

4. Apparitions of Mary
   Aim: to tell the story of at least one of the apparitions of Mary.
   Activities: see activities 2, 6, and 7.

5. Review
   Aim: to review this week's material.
   Activities: review game, quiz.

Notes:

CHAPTER 30

Unto Everlasting Life

Background Reading for the Teacher:

Lawler, pp. 511−524, 525−539.
Hardon, pp. 254−280.

Aims:

The students should be able to list the Last Things; to explain the resurrection of the body.

Materials Needed:

A picture of the Last Judgment, Activity Book.

Activities

1. Read and discuss Chapter 30 in class, pp. 113−115.

2. Explain what it means if a saint's body is incorrupt (see *The Incorruptibles* by Joan Cruz, published by Tan Books).

3. Review Christ's Resurrection and discuss the qualities of a glorified body.

4. Discuss and give a drill on the catechism questions, pp. 116−117.

5. Show the students a picture of the Last Judgment, such as the picture on p. 114 in the text or Michelangelo's *Last Judgment*. Discuss the various aspects: Christ in judgment, people rising from the dead, some being taken up to heaven, others being dragged into hell by demons, etc.

Lesson Plan for a One-day Presentation

1. Pray.

2. Read and discuss Chapter 30, pp. 113−115.

3. Review Christ's Resurrection and discuss the qualities of a glorified body.

4. Tell the story of saints whose bodies are incorrupt (for example, St. Bernadette, St. Catherine Labouré, or Blessed Margaret of Castello).

5. Show the students a picture of the Last Judgment (see activity 5).

6. Discuss and give a drill on the catechism questions on pp. 116−117 in the text (use flash cards or a game).

7. Review the course. You may want to give a whole lesson to review.

8. Give a comprehensive test.

9. Pray.

Suggested Schedule for a Five-day Presentation

1. Death and judgment
   Aim: to list and explain the four Last Things.
   Activities: see activities 1 and 5.

2. Heaven, hell, and purgatory
   Aim: to list and explain the four Last Things.
   Activities: see activities 1 and 4.

3. Resurrection of the body
   Aim: to explain the resurrection of the body.
   Activities: see activities 2 and 3.

4. Review
   Aim: to review the material covered in this course.
   Activities: serious review and review games.

5. Review
   Aim: see day 4.
   Activities: test. You may wish to devote a whole week to review the course.

Notes:

Appendix

LESSON PLAN OVERVIEW

To plan the year's course, write a title or phrase for the material you are going to cover in a week's time and the pages where the material can be found in the textbook. For example: 1. *Introduction, pp. 9–11.*

1. _____
   _____

2. _____
   _____

3. _____
   _____

4. _____
   _____

5. _____
   _____

6. _____
   _____

7. _____
   _____

8. _____
   _____

9. _____
   _____

10. _____
    _____

11. _____
    _____

12. _____
    _____

13. _____
    _____

14. _____
    _____

15. _____
    _____

16. _____
    _____

17. _____
    _____

18. _____
    _____

19. _____
    _____

20. _____
    _____

21. _____

22. _____

23. _____

24. _____

25. _____

26. _____

27. _____

28. _____

29. _____

30. _____

31. _____

32. _____

33. _____

34. _____

35. _____

36. _____

37. _____

38. _____

39. _____

40. _____

BASIC TRUTHS OF THE CHRISTIAN FAITH

1. *Who created us?*
   God created us.

2. *Who is God?*
   God is the all-perfect Being, Creator and Lord of heaven and earth.

3. *What does "all-perfect" mean?*
   "All-perfect" means that every perfection is found in God, without defect and without limit; in other words it means that he is infinite power, wisdom and goodness.

4. *What does "Creator" mean?*
   "Creator" means that God made all things out of nothing.

5. *What does "Lord" mean?*
   "Lord" means that God is the absolute master of all things.

6. *Does God have a body as we have?*
   No, God does not have a body, for he is a perfectly pure spirit.

7. *Where is God?*
   God is in heaven, on earth, and in every place: he is the unlimited Being.

8. *Has God always existed?*
   Yes, God always has been and always will be: he is the eternal Being.

9. *Does God know all things?*
   Yes, God knows all things, even our thoughts: he is all-knowing.

10. *Can God do all things?*
    God can do all that he wills to do: he is the all-powerful one.

11. *Can God do also something evil?*
    No, God cannot do evil, because he cannot will evil, for he is infinite goodness. But he tolerates evil in order to leave creatures free, and he knows how to bring good even out of evil.

12. *Does God take care of created things?*
    Yes, God takes care of created things and exercises providence over them; he preserves them in existence and directs all of them toward their own proper purposes with infinite wisdom, goodness, and justice.

13. *What purpose did God have in mind when he created us?*
    God created us to know him, to love him and to serve him in this life, and then to enjoy him in the next life, in heaven.

14. *What is heaven?*
    Heaven is the eternal enjoyment of God, who is our happiness, and the enjoyment of all other good things in him, without any evil.

15. *Who merits heaven?*
    Every good person merits heaven—that is, he who loves God, serves him faithfully and dies in his grace.

16. *What do the wicked deserve who do not serve God and who die in mortal sin?*
    The wicked who do not serve God and who die in mortal sin merit hell.

17. *What is hell?*
    Hell is the eternal suffering of the loss of God, who is our happiness. This means a deep and real personal suffering.

18. *Why does God reward the good and punish the wicked?*

God rewards the good and punishes the wicked because he is infinite justice.

19. *Is there only one God?*
There is only one God, but in three equal and distinct Persons, who are the most Holy Trinity.

20. *What are the three Persons of the Holy Trinity called?*
The three Persons of the Holy Trinity are called the Father, the Son, and the Holy Spirit.

21. *Of the three Persons of the Holy Trinity, was one "incarnate", that is, made man?*
Yes, the Second Person, God the Son, became "incarnate", that is, was made man.

22. *What is the Son of God made man called?*
The Son of God made man is called Jesus Christ.

23. *Who is Jesus Christ?*
Jesus Christ is the Second Person of the most Holy Trinity, that is, the Son of God made man.

24. *Is Jesus Christ God and man?*
Yes, Jesus Christ is true God and true man.

25. *Why did the Son of God become man?*
The Son of God became man to save us, that is, to redeem us from sin and to regain heaven for us.

26. *What did Jesus Christ do to save us?*
To save us, Jesus Christ made satisfaction for our sins by suffering and sacrificing himself on the cross, and he taught us how to live according to God's laws.

27. *What must we do to live according to God's laws?*
To live according to God's laws we must believe the truths which he has revealed and observe his commandments, with the help of his grace, which we obtain by means of the sacraments and prayer.

REVIEW GAMES

Review games are valuable in helping the students to remember the lesson. Students are usually more motivated to memorize things to win a game than to complete a straight memorization assignment. Games can also be used to build confidence (when the teacher gauges the questions to the ability of each student) and cooperation among the students. Often times, the reward of winning is enough for students. However, you might want to give little prizes such as holy cards or medals, etc. The games below will be marked according to the grade level at which they work best: $1° =$ grades $1-3$; $2° = 4-6$; and $3° = 7-8$.

Bible Baseball 1°, 2°

1. Set up bases around the room.

2. Pick teams.

3. Ask a question of a student on one of the teams. If he gets the answer, the student goes to first base and the next student is up for a question. If he misses the answer, he is out. The next teammate must answer the same question. If three students on the same team cannot answer the question or if three questions are missed their team is out and the other team is up.

4. Points are received for ''home runs'', that is, when a student has gotten to all three bases and reached home base.

Tic Tac Toe 1°, 2°

1. Pick sides. ''X'' goes first.

2. Draw grid on the chalkboard.

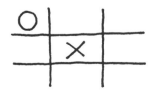

3. Ask a question of a student on the first team. If he answers it correctly, his team chooses where to put the ''X''. If he answers incorrectly, the other team has a chance to answer the question. If the ''O'' team answers correctly, they can choose where to put the ''O'', and then they get their turn. If they answer incorrectly, they merely get their normal turn.

4. The team that gets three ''X's'', or three ''O's'' in a row wins the round. Losers start the next round.

Peek-a-Boo 2°, 3°

1. Pick sides.

2. A student from one team stands at the front of the room with his back to the chalkboard.

3. The teacher writes a word on the board.

4. Teammates can give only one clue to the member at the board. The student at the board chooses which of his teammates will give the clue. A different clue-giver must be chosen for each word.

5. If the student says the word on the board, his team gets a point and the next member

of the team gets a chance at the board. If he fails to say the word, the other team gets to play.

Credo 2°, 3°

(This game takes a long time.)

1. Each student plays for himself.

2. Have each student fold a piece of paper in half and cut at the fold.

3. On one half sheet of paper, draw a "CREDO" card (see illustration).

4. Write 25 – 30 words on the board that relate to the material that you are reviewing; have the students write fill-in-the-blank questions for each word. Assign which word(s) each student will write a question for, so that all the words have a question. Each question should be on a separate piece of paper.

5. Have the students write a word from the board into every box on their "CREDO" cards. No repeats. The middle box is a FREE space.

6. Collect the questions from the students. Mix them up and read a question aloud, twice. If the student has the word on his "CREDO" card, he draws a line through the word, but is careful not to make it unreadable, so that the teacher can check

it if the student wins. Proceed as with a BINGO game.

7. When a student gets a row or black out or four corners he says, "Credo!" If all the words the student crossed out were correct, he must say the words and the questions to the class before he wins.

Modified "Hangman" 2°, 3°

1. Pick teams (2 or more).

2. Think of a message (or have a list ready beforehand). For example: GOD IS GOOD.

3. Write the spaces for the message on the chalkboard. __ __ __ / __ __ / __ __ __ __ __.

4. A member from the first team guesses a letter. If he is correct, the team gets a point for every time the letter occurs, for example: if he had guessed a "G" his team would get 2 points (G __ __ / __ __ / G __ __ __) and another member of his team gets to guess the next letter. If he is wrong, write the letter on the board as a letter already used. The turn goes to the next team.

5. If anyone on any team can guess the message before all the letters are in place, he may interrupt and give the answer. His team receives 5 bonus points. If the student guesses incorrectly, his team has 5 points taken away.

6. The team that reaches 100 (or 50, or 25, etc.) first wins. The game can also be played with a time limit instead of a point limit.

Divine Pursuit 2°, 3°

Materials: game board (see illustration), a die, tokens (such as figurines of Jesus, Mary and the saints), plastic or paper chips, cards with catechism questions and answers written on them.

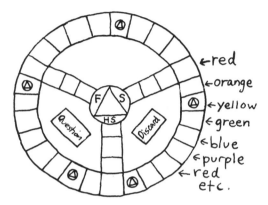

←red
←orange
←yellow
←green
←blue
←purple
←red
etc.

Note: Use six colors for the squares, using each color in succession around the circle and straight paths.

1. Each player (or team) rolls the die. The lowest roll is first. The player to the left is next, etc. Tokens start at the center of the board.

2. To take a turn, roll the die and move the number of spaces indicated on the die. If the person lands on a yellow space, another player draws and asks a question. If the player cannot answer, his turn ends. The correct answer is read aloud and the card put in the discard pile. If the player answers correctly, he receives a red chip and his turn ends. If the player lands on a square of any other color, his turn is over.

3. When a player has obtained three chips, he moves to the center, which must be reached by an exact roll. The player must then answer a question from the pile. If he answers correctly, he has won the game. If not, the player must leave the center on the next turn, and return for another question.

4. When no more questions are left in the question pile, shuffle the discard pile and it will become the question pile again.

DRAMATIZATION

Dramatization of a scene from Scripture, or the Rosary, etc., helps the students to use all their faculties and senses in learning. For the younger children, you might have to write and produce the play yourself, but older children (grades 3−8) can make and produce the play themselves. Thus, the students use their imagination and creativity as well as their senses. Below are three ways you can dramatize a scene.

Popsicle Stick Puppets and Shoe Box Theater

The puppets are easily made from popsicle sticks and either felt, construction paper, or cut out pictures. For example:

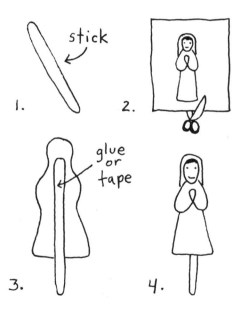

(the slot toward the top will be where you insert the puppets; the slot toward the bottom will be for inserting the backdrop, or scenery).

For the theater, take a large shoe box and cut two slots, one toward the top of the box on one of the long sides, and the other toward the bottom of the box on the opposite long side

Masks

To identify the different characters in a play without having to make elaborate costumes, it is quite easy to make masks. For example, if you wanted to dramatize the temptation and fall of man, you could make the following masks out of paper and have the students color them, or make them out of construction paper.

EVE ADAM GOD SERPENT ANGEL

To show the change from perfect happiness to the fallen state of Adam and Eve, or the original delight of Satan at man's fall, then disappointment at God's promise, make the masks reversible. The masks may be hand-held and then flipped at the proper time during the skit. For example:

Adam before the Fall.

Adam after the Fall

Costumes and Props

Costumes do not have to be elaborate to be effective. An old sheet, bathrobe, or remnants of material are usually all you need. If you need a crown and a miter these can be made out of construction paper and sized to fit the head of the actor. For example:

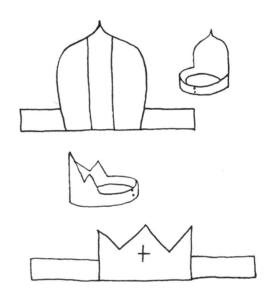

Beards too are easily made of paper, then hooked around the ears:

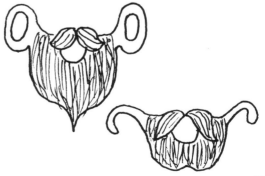

99

Swords can be cut out from cardboard and covered with aluminum foil, and chains can be made by linking paper strips together. (Chains and swords might be used for a play on Joan of Arc or on Joseph being sold into slavery, etc.)

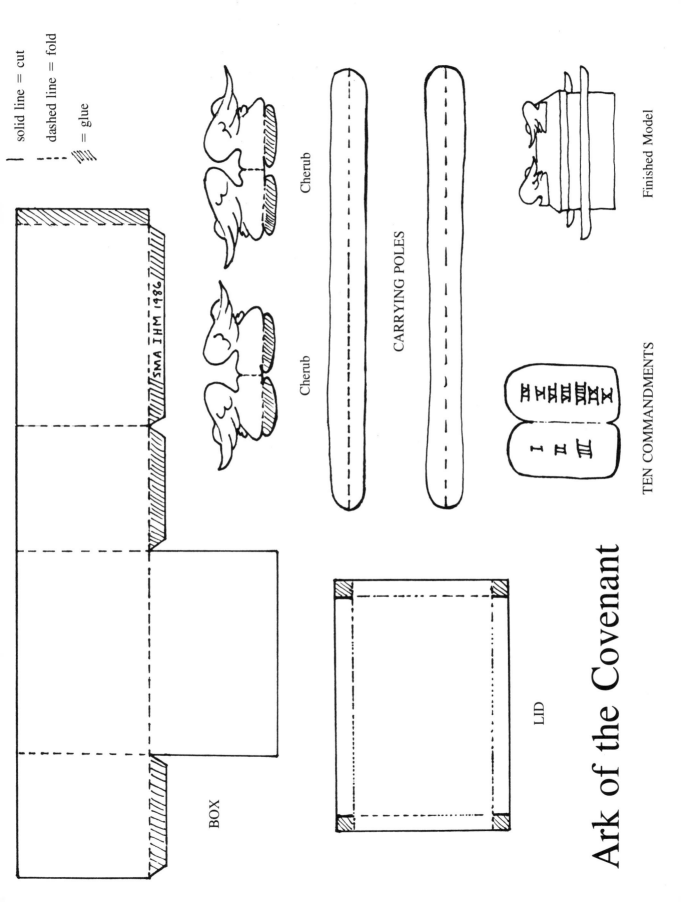

solid line = cut

dashed line = fold

▨ = glue

Cherub

Cherub

SMA IHM 1986

BOX

CARRYING POLES

LID

Finished Model

TEN COMMANDMENTS

Ark of the Covenant

"Matchbox" Nativity

Color.
Cut out.
Fold tabs of BACK forward.
Insert MIDDLE in the "A" slots on the tabs of the BACK.
Insert FRONT in the "B" slots.
Fold ROOF and place it on top of the stable.

Assembled

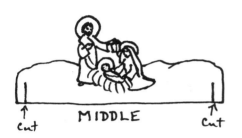

MIDDLE   Cut   Cut

JMA, IHM 1986

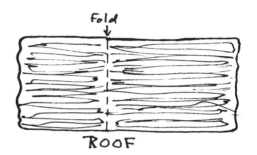

Fold

ROOF

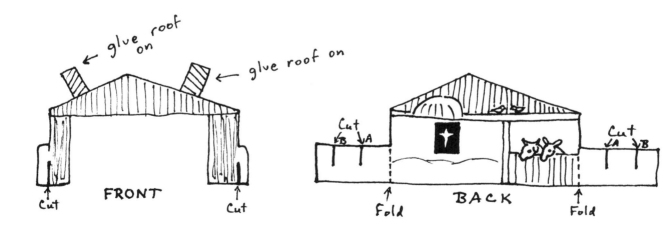

glue roof on   glue roof on

FRONT   Cut   Cut

Cut ↓B ↓A   Cut ↓A ↓B

BACK

Fold   Fold

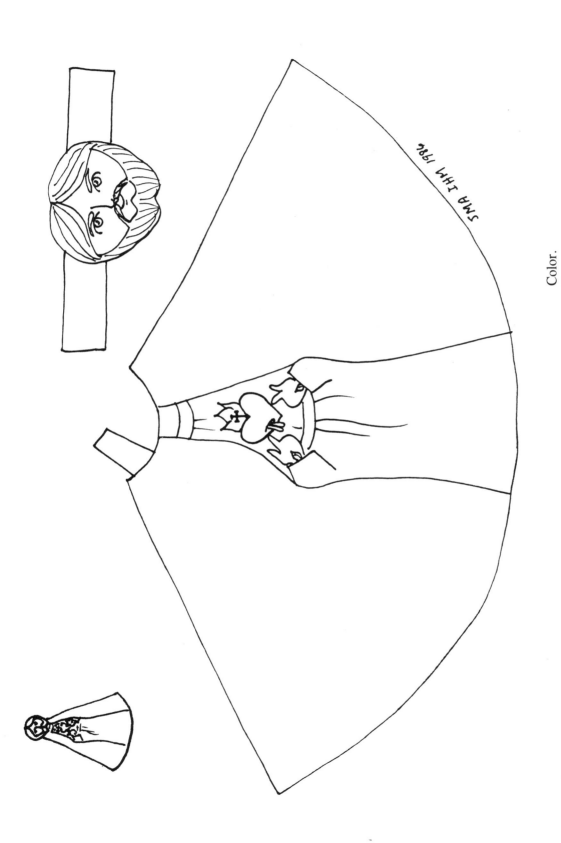

Color.
Cut.
Roll the body into a cone and glue or tape.
Glue tabs of the head together.
Glue head to the tab on the body.

SMA IHM 1984

Sacred Heart Figurine

Grade 5 Activity Book Answer Key

N.B.: Many of the questions require the student to give an answer in his own words. Where specific doctrinal or historical points that the student is expected to learn in this course of studies are looked for, suggested answers (or outlines) are provided to the teacher. In other places, the student is expected to write a response for which no specific answer is needed. A note is provided to indicate that answers will vary.

Students should answer in complete sentences.

Chapter 1

I.

The Apostles' Creed states that:

1. There is a God, the Father Almighty, Creator of heaven and earth.
2. Jesus Christ is his only Son, Our Lord.
3. Jesus was conceived by the Holy Spirit and born of the Virgin Mary.
4. Jesus suffered under Pontius Pilate, was crucified, died, and was buried.
5. Jesus descended into hell, the third day he arose again from the dead.
6. Jesus ascended into heaven, sits at the right hand of God, the Father Almighty.
7. From thence he shall come to judge the living and the dead.
8. Catholics believe in the Holy Spirit.
9. Catholics believe in the Holy Catholic Church and the Communion of Saints.
10. Catholics believe in the forgiveness of sins.
11. Catholics believe in the resurrection of the body.
12. Catholics believe in life everlasting.

II.

1. We express our belief in the Trinity: God, the Father; God, the Son; and God, the Holy Spirit, by the words that we use to accompany our actions.
2. We express our belief in the Passion and death of Jesus Christ by tracing the cross with our hand.

Chapter 2

I. Answers will vary. Examples:

Mark 1:10−11: All three persons of the trinity are shown to those present at the baptism of Jesus. The Father claims him as his Son.

Matthew 28:19: Jesus tells his disciples to teach all nations about the Unity and Trinity of God. He tells them to baptize the people when they come to a belief in the name of the Father, the Son, and the Holy Spirit.

John 16:5−15: Jesus speaks of the work of the Trinity in man's life. The Father sent Jesus to redeem man, just as Jesus will send the Holy Spirit to guide man.

II.

Shamrock: although there are three distinct parts to the shamrock, taken together they make one leaf.

Equilateral triangle: each side of the triangle is equal to the other, all three sides make the triangle a triangle.

Chapter 3

Answers will vary. Examples:

I.

Create means to bring something into being out of nothing. Man can be said to create things like art or clothes, but he makes these things from tools that he has around him. Only God can truly create something out of nothing like Heaven and earth, angels and animals.

II.

God exists: We can know that God exists because things like the universe, man, animals, plants, and earth exist. They cannot exist from nothing. God has created them.

God is all-powerful: We can know that God is all-powerful by recognizing the complexity and beauty of the universe, of humans, animals, and plants.

God is wise: We can know that God is wise by noticing how the world works in harmony, for example, a squirrel burying an oak seed so an oak tree will grow or the earth's rotation to allow night and day.

God is good: We can see that God is good because of the beauty that surrounds us in nature like the sea, the sky, the animals, and because of the beauty in good people like parents, grandparents and friends.

Chapter 4

Genesis 22:1−19: An angel told Abraham that due to his faith, Isaac would be spared and Abraham's descendants would be a blessed nation.

Judges 13:1−14: An angel told Manoah's wife that although she was barren, she will have a son who will deliver the Israelites from the Philistines.

Tobit 5:1−6 and Tobit 12: The angel Raphael disguised himself as a young man. He assures Tobiah that he will lead him to Media to recover the debt that is owed to Tobiah's parents.

Luke 1:5−23: The angel Gabriel told Zacharias that his wife would bear a son who would turn people's hearts to God. He also told Zacharias that for not believing he would be struck dumb until this is performed.

Luke 1:26−38: The angel Gabriel told Mary that through the power of the Holy Spirit she shall conceive a child. That her child, Jesus, will reign on earth and in Heaven. He told her that Elizabeth will have a son also.

Luke 2:8−20: The angels announced the good news of Jesus' birth to the shepherds.

Matthew 2:13−23: An angel told Joseph to flee into Egypt to avoid the slaughter of the innocents by Herod. When Herod died, the angel told Joseph to return to his homeland.

Acts 12:1−11: An angel came to deliver Peter from prison out of the hand of Herod.

Chapter 5

I. Answers will vary. Example:

Man is made in the image and likeness of God in that we have a mind and a freedom of choice. We also have the capacity to love others as God loves us. God also gave man dominion over other living creatures as God has dominion over all that is created.

II.

Angelic: Man has his spiritual life in common with the angels. He can think, know, and freely choose what is good or evil. Also, a man's soul will never die because it is immortal like the angels.

Animal: Man shares some things with animals because he has a body. He can feel things, he has the senses of sight, hearing, touch, taste, and smell. He needs food, air, and water to survive like animals.

Vegetative: Man shares some things with the vegetative since he has a body. Man and vegetation have the processes of life, such as growth and death, in common.

Chapter 6

Answers will vary. Examples:

I.

before the Fall:
life free from pain, sickness, death
life in harmony with living creatures
sanctifying grace of God
knew God as a friend
confident of eternal life with God

after the Fall:
life with pain, sickness, death
life with exhausting work
life of ignorance
no hope of eternal life in Heaven by their own efforts

II.

before Baptism:
life without the graces of Christ's death
life with original sin
souls without sanctifying grace
life not as God's children

after Baptism:
life with graces of Christ's death
original sin is removed
souls filled with sanctifying grace
life as God's children

Chapter 7

I.

1. Abraham is called "Our Father in Faith" because of the great faith he had in God. At God's command, he moved to an unfamiliar land and was ready to sacrifice his only beloved son, Isaac.

2. Abraham is also called "Our Father in Faith" because his descendants were the chosen people

who had faith in God and received his special care and attention in return. This group would prepare the world for the Messiah who would save man from sin and bring salvation.

II.

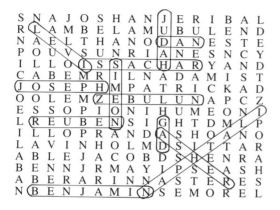

Judah, Issachar, Levi, Dan, Simeon, Zebulun, Reuben, Gad, Asher, Benjamin, Naphtali, Joseph.

Chapter 8

8; 5; 2; 9; 4; 7; 1; 6; 3.

II. Answers will vary.

Chapter 9

I.

Across:
1. Ark of the Covenant
2. covenant
3. Moses

Down:
4. manna
5. David
6. Ten Commandments
7. Mount Sinai

II.

1. I am the Lord your God; you shall not have strange gods before me.
2. You shall not take the Name of the Lord your God in vain.
3. Remember to keep holy the Lord's Day.
4. Honor your father and mother.
5. You shall not kill.
6. You shall not commit adultery.
7. You shall not steal.
8. You shall not bear false witness against your neighbor.
9. You shall not covet your neighbor's wife.
10. You shall not covet your neighbor's goods.

Chapter 10

I.

I am the voice of one crying in the wilderness, "Make straight the way for the Lord."

II.

Mark with "P" 1; 3; 5; 6.

Chapter 11

I.

soul; Savior; favor; generations; great; holy; mercy; strength; proud; mighty; lifted; hungry; rich; aid; promise; fathers; Abraham.

II.

Gabriel: The archangel Gabriel told Zachariah that his wife would bear a son in her old age. The son would be John the Baptist. Gabriel also announced to Mary that she would conceive a son, the Son of God.

Mary: Mary was chosen by God to be the Mother of Jesus, God's own Son. She was told that she would conceive the child by the power of the Holy Spirit.

Zachariah: The angel Gabriel revealed to Zachariah that his wife would bear a son even though she was so old. Since Zachariah answered the angel's message without belief, he was struck dumb until the baby was born as proof of God's power.

Elizabeth: At an old age, Elizabeth conceived a son. Gabriel revealed that her son, John the Baptist, would be a great prophet and turn the hearts of many back to God.

John the Baptist: John the Baptist was a great prophet. He turned many people's hearts back to God.

Joseph: Joseph was engaged to Mary when the angel announced that she was chosen to be the Mother of God's own Son. He was the protector of Jesus and Mary.

Chapter 12

Gabriel: Gabriel the archangel announced to Mary that because she was favored by God, she would conceive God's own Son through the power of the Holy Spirit.

Mary: Mary accepted the words of the angel and the will of God with great faith.

Elizabeth: Elizabeth was filled with the Holy Spirit when Mary visited her. She praised Mary as the Mother of God.

Zachariah: As soon as his son was born, Zachariah believed what the angel had told him. Zachariah praised God for sending this son who would prepare the way of the Lord.

angel: The angel appeared to shepherds to announce the birth of Jesus, the Savior.

Simeon: Empowered by the Holy Spirit, Simeon recognized Jesus as the Savior.

Chapter 13

1. Annunciation (Nazareth)
2. Visitation (hill country of Judea—Ain Karim)
3. the birth of Jesus (Bethlehem)
4. Presentation of Jesus (Jerusalem)
5. flight into Egypt
6. return from Egypt
7. where the Holy Family settled (Nazareth)
8. finding in the Temple (Jerusalem)

Chapter 14

"If you are the Son of God command these stones to become loaves of bread."

—*matches with*—

"Man does not live by bread alone but by every word that proceeds from the mouth of God."

"If you are the Son of God throw yourself down; for it is written, 'He will give his angels charge of you.'"

—*matches with*—

"You shall not tempt the Lord your God."

"All these [kingdoms of the world] I will give you if you will fall down and worship me."

—*matches with*—

"You shall worship the Lord your God and him only shall you serve."

Chapter 15

Luke 8:22−25: the calming of the storm
Matthew 15:32−38: the multiplication of the loaves and fishes
John 11:17−44: the raising of Lazarus
Matthew 17:1−8: the Transfiguration
Luke 8:26−33: the casting out of devils
Matthew 9:27−31: the curing of the blind men

II.
1. F; 2. T; 3. F; 4. T; 5. F; 6. T.

Chapter 16

I.

Across:	*Down*:
1. Prodigal Son	4. forgiveness
2. Pharisees	5. sinners
3. repent	6. sorrow
	7. Zacchaeus

II.
The story of the Prodigal Son tells us of God's unconditional, never-ending love for man. Even though the son abandoned the father to live a life of sin, the father rejoiced at his son's return. The father forgave the son for he repented of his ways and returned to live in the father's love.

Chapter 17

John 11:25−26 — D
John 7:37−39 — D
Mark 11:15−16 — H
John 6:41−53 — D
John 11:33−36 — H

Matthew 21:18 — H
Mark 1:35 — H
Mark 6:3 — H
Luke 3:22 — D
Luke 8:26−33 — D

Chapter 18

1. F; 2. T; 3. F; 4. F; 5. T.

II.

mistaken Messiah
Jesus would:
spend time with important leaders
be a man
be a holy leader

Jesus as the true Messiah
Jesus:
spent time with ordinary people
was both a man and God
was rejected by the important leaders of the Jews

Chapter 19

I.

Across:	Down:
1. Blessed	3. wine
2. Body	4. Calvary
3. washed	7. Palm
4. Communion	9. cross
5. Lord	10. Supper
6. Friday	11. Holy
7. Passover	12. Blood
8. bread	13. death

II.

First mystery: The first Sorrowful Mystery is the Agony in the Garden. Jesus' prayer in the garden of Gethsemane was filled with sorrow and distress yet he accepted his Father's will. Jesus became angry that his disciples could not stay awake with him (Matthew 26:36—44).

Second mystery: The second Sorrowful Mystery is the Scourging at the Pillar. After Jesus was sentenced to death, Pilate sent Jesus to be scourged (John 19:1).

Third mystery: The third Sorrowful Mystery is the Crowning with Thorns. Soldiers stripped Jesus and wrapped a scarlet cloak on him. Then they wove a crown of thorns on his head. They mocked him, spat at him and struck him on the head (Matthew 27:27—31).

Fourth mystery: The fourth Sorrowful Mystery is the Carrying of the Cross. Jesus carried the cross by himself to Golgotha or the Place of the Skull (John 19:17).

Fifth mystery: The fifth Sorrowful Mystery is the Crucifixion. Jesus was crucified at Golgotha with two others (John 19:18).

Chapter 20

I.

Sacrifice of Abel

1. Abel is the one who offers the sacrifice.
2. The offering of the sacrifice is the firstlings of his flock.
3. Abel offered this sacrifice out of worship to God.
4. The Lord respected Abel and his offering.

Sacrifice of Melchizedek

1. Melchizedek is the priest who offers the sacrifice.
2. The offering is of bread and wine.
3. Melchizedek offered this sacrifice in thanks to God.
4. The Lord delivered him and his people from their enemies.

Sacrifice of Abraham

1. Abraham is the one who offers the sacrifice.
2. The offering of the sacrifice is a ram.
3. Abraham offered this sacrifice out of thanksgiving and worship.
4. The Lord blessed Abraham's seed for his great faith.

Sacrifice of the Israelites

1. A priest is the one who offers the sacrifice for the Israelites.
2. The offering of the sacrifice is a bull without blemish.
3. The priest offers this sacrifice in worship of the Lord.
4. If the priest follows God's instructions, the offering will be of a sweet savor unto the Lord.

II.

Sacrifice of the Cross	Sacrifice of the Mass
Jesus	priest
Jesus	Jesus and ourselves
sacrifice for sin	to perpetuate the redemptive act
salvation from eternal death for all mankind	give ourselves as a gift to God
bloody death on the cross	unbloody offering

Chapter 21

lamb with a banner: Christ as the Lamb of God, symbolic of the sacrifice/victim offered for our sins, has been triumphant over death—banner as a sign of victory

butterfly: Symbol of the Resurrection and eternal life because the caterpillar dies and is transformed into a butterfly.

grain of wheat: Symbolic of Christ dying to bring us new life as the single grain of wheat must be buried to bring forth more new wheat.

rising sun: Symbolic of Christ overcoming darkness of sin and death as rising sun overcomes darkness of night.

candle: Christ is seen as the light of the world.

Chapter 22

1. Holy Spirit; 2. Pope; 3. Thomas; 4. Heaven; 5. Apostles, forgive; 6. resurrection; 7. Olivet; 8. come.

II.

Jesus.	The apostles.
Thomas.	The other apostles.
Jesus.	Thomas.
Peter.	Jesus.
Jesus.	Peter.
An angel.	The apostles.

Chapter 23

dove: The Holy Spirit appeared in the form of a dove at Christ's baptism in all four Gospels.

fire: Tongues of fire appeared and rested on the apostle's heads. This was pone sign to the apostles that the Holy Spirit had come.

wind: the roar of wind accompanied the descent of the Holy Spirit upon the apostles. The noise of the wind brought an audience to witness the workings of the Holy Spirit in the apostles.

II.

We believe in the Holy Spirit,

the *Lord*,

the *Giver of Life*,

who *proceeds from the Father and the Son*.

With *the Father and the Son he is worshipped and glorified*.

He *has spoken through the prophets*.

The first phrase affirms belief in God, the Holy Spirit.

The second phrase affirms that the Holy Spirit is God.

The third phrase refers to the Holy Spirit's role in giving life to Jesus in Mary's womb. It also refers to the Holy Spirit's role in beginning the preaching life of the apostles after Jesus left them.

The fourth phrase affirms belief that the Holy Spirit is actually the Love that God the Father and God the Son have for one another. Thus, the Creed continues in the second sentence to affirm belief that this Love is so perfect and so great that it is another Person, equal to the Father and the Son. Since the Holy Spirit is equal to the Father and Son, he is worshipped and glorified as the third Person of the Holy Trinity. Finally, the last sentence refers to the Holy Spirit's work of inspiration of the prophets and the writers of sacred Scripture.

Chapter 24

1. Apostles	6. Pope
2. Pentecost	7. Christ
3. founder	8. members
4. Peter	9. Communion of
5. Mystical Body	Saints

```
S A I N T I N F A P O S T O L I C T
C O M M U N I O N O F S A I N T S O
A H N D P V L U G P O E P O Z O E S
C H R I S I A N E E L A O V C S A I
R O I A T C D L P L O S E N T A D
I P S K S E N E S T O N T B X O L I
F E E P E D E R A P W N L O D R E S
I M A R Y S E N D O E Y E D R A L C
C R E A T B N W R P A U S Y D U H I
E V E O M I J O S E P H S A R A H P
S A V E H O L Y S P I R I T I X T L
A N M Y S T I C A L B O D Y A N D E
```

Chapter 25

I.

one: The Church is one because all Catholics in the world share the exact same beliefs about our salvation.

holy: The Church is holy because Jesus who founded it and the Holy Spirit who guides it are holy, and its aim is to make all members holy.

catholic: The Church is catholic because the Church is for all men united in a brotherhood of faith.

apostolic: The Church is apostolic because the spiritual leaders trace their powers back to the apostles who were guided by the Holy Spirit.

II.

Matthew 21:42: Jesus as cornerstone

Acts 4:11: Jesus as cornerstone

1 Corinthians 3:9—17: We are part of the building (members of the Church)

Ephesians 2:19—22: Fellow members, apostles and prophets are foundations of the Church

1 Peter 2:4 −8: each stone, each member is precious

We learn that the Catholic faith began with one man Jesus. We learn that Jesus is the foundation of the Church. He set the supreme example of faith and human action for all Christians to follow. The Church is built around the example of Jesus, each person working with the other to keep the structure together.

Chapter 26

bishop . . . a leader in the Church who is a successor to the apostles

Pope . . . the supreme teacher and leader of the Church, the successor of Peter; he holds the place of Jesus in the Church on earth

cardinal . . . a person, usually a bishop, whom the Pope has chosen to belong to a special group of advisors who elect new popes

diocese . . . a territory over which a bishop rules

priest . . . a man who has special powers through the sacrament of Holy Orders to offer Mass and administer the other sacraments

pastor . . . the priest in charge of a parish

precepts of the Church . . . special laws made by the Church

deacon . . . a man ordained to serve in the ministry of the Word, of the liturgy, and of charity

parish . . . a community of Catholics who worship together in the same church and are led by a pastor

Chapter 27

I.

Go and teach all nations.

The harvest is indeed great, but the laborers are few; pray therefore the Lord of the harvest to send forth laborers into his harvest.

II.

Pope: These two directives ask the Pope to proclaim the truths of the faith to all nations.

bishop: The two directives ask bishops to proclaim the truths of the faith to those of all nations, especially those in his diocese.

priest: The two directives ask priests to proclaim the truths of the faith to those people to whom he preaches.

religious sister or brother: The two directives ask brothers and sisters to continuously pray to the Lord for the souls to become laborers.

laity: The two directives ask the laity to pray so that they may be worthy as laborers. It also asks them to teach and to pray for those who could become laborers.

Chapter 28

I.

```
G R A C E F K N O T H S D I O C E S E
R A N O S A V I O R T H W C H O M E N
A B I S H O P V N I F O M X C N I O T
C A T O L N D Y P A R I S H F A L T S
I P A R T E X I S T I F R I E I N D S
O T E U C H A R I S T R Y   P R A Y E
U I U A N O O L S B H I Q U E M A S T
S S C A P P O L I N G S U L J A S I A
A M H P E E K L Y O S T R A N T O C K
A N O I N T I N G O F T H E S I C K E
J A R N A M A M B L R O U N D O D Y P
S T I N N I N G F X C D E A C N O L E
I O T Y C O M M U N I T E J O U R N D
S A S A E R A M E N M A T R I M O N Y
A L S A C R E D I N E R E Y S W X L S
```

II.

1. The first step for making a good confession is examination of conscience.
2. The second step is to be sorry for your sins.
3. The third step is to make the decision not to sin again.
4. The fourth step is to confess your sins to the priest.
5. The fifth step is to do the penance that the priest gives you.

Chapter 29

Annunciation: The Annunciation commemorates the angel's announcement to Mary that she would be the Mother of God. The feast is celebrated March 25.

Assumption: The Assumption commemorates when Mary was assumed into Heaven body and soul. The feast is celebrated August 15.

Queenship of Mary: The Queenship of Mary commemorates Mary as exalted by God above all other creatures, second only to her Son, Christ. This feast is August 22.

Immaculate Conception: The Immaculate Conception commemorates Mary's conception, in which she was free from original sin. The feast is December 8.

Solemnity of Mary, Mother of God: The Solemnity of Mary commemorates Mary's role in salvation history as the Mother of God. This feast is on January 1.

Visitation: The Visitation commemorates Mary's visit to Elizabeth. The Visitation is celebrated on May 31.

Birth of Mary: This feast commemorates Mary's birth. The feast is celebrated on the 8th of September.

Our Lady of Guadalupe: The feast of Our Lady of Guadalupe commemorates Mary's appearance in Tepeyac, Mexico. The feast is celebrated December 12.

Presentation of the Blessed Virgin Mary: This feast recalls the tradition that Mary was presented to God by her parents in the temple. It is celebrated on November 21.

Our Lady of Lourdes: The feast of Our Lady of Lourdes commemorates the appearance of Mary in Lourdes, France. The feast is celebrated February 11.

Our Lady of Mount Carmel: This feast commemorates the founding of the Carmelite Order under the patronage of Mary. It is celebrated July 16.

Our Lady of the Rosary: This feast celebrates the victory of the Christians at the battle of Lepanto through the aid of Mary invoked through the prayer of the Rosary. It is celebrated on October 7.

Immaculate Heart of Mary: This feast celebrates the great and pure love Mary has for God and for us. It is a movable feast, celebrated the Saturday following the second Sunday after Pentecost, or the day after the feast of the Sacred Heart.

Chapter 30

I.

Across:
1. Eternal
2. resurrection
3. hell
4. coming

Down:
5. Death
6. Purgatory
7. general
8. particular
9. Heaven

II.

Answers will vary.